Rona
the distant
island

Michael Robson

The publishers acknowledge financial subsidy from The Scottish Arts
Council towards the publication of this volume.

The publishers are also grateful for financial assistance from The Nature
Conservancy Council for Scotland.

First published in Scotland in 1991 by Acair Ltd, Unit 8A, 7 James
Street, Stornoway, Isle of Lewis.

Designed by Acair Ltd.
Cover photograph by Sam Maynard.
Printed by Highland Printers, Inverness.

ISBN 0 86152 867 0 (Hardback)
ISBN 0 86152 823 9 (Paperback)

*The Rona cross, pictured in the cover photograph and repeated in the
illustration at the start of each Part in the text, is described on page 20.*

RONA

The Distant Island

Michael Robson

acair

1991

Norman MacKay (Tormod Beag), Skigersta, descended from Rona families and with much knowledge of the island and its people.

(photo. Comunn Eachdraidh Nis Collection)

Author's Foreword and Acknowledgements

Rona seems always to have been associated with the district of Ness in the island of Lewis. After 1700, and possibly before, the inhabitants were really Ness people of Ness origin, and their descendants today live in the Ness villages. Anyone seeking to tell the story of Rona must surely turn, as Martin Martin did long ago, to the Ness community for help and information which can be found nowhere else.

In trying to find out about Rona it is of course essential to look at earlier maps, papers and books, even those books which contain incorrect details and those maps which show two islands of Rona instead of one and put them both in the wrong part of the sea. But the present book would not have been written without the knowledge so willingly and patiently shared in conversation at gable-ends out of the wind and at cosy firesides in Habost, Cross, Fivepenny and indeed everywhere between Dell and Eoropie. Those whose names appear below, some of them not in or even belonging to Ness, have in one way or another made the story possible, and among them are a few who, like Angus Gunn over a century ago, happened to know more than most and to possess the rare gift of expressing themselves in memorable words. Putting together this account of Rona brought therefore an unexpected reward — the happy recollection of Am Puilean out on the croft in a summer midnight talking above the corncrake in the grass, of Stugan sitting upright with the cap on telling of *am bathadh mor*, the great drowning, of Tormod Beag by the fireside in Skigersta going through the generations of Mackays and Macdonalds, and of Snagaidh with his gentle yet eager interest and pleasure in recollecting journeys to Rona. And of others too — all holding their special place in the long list of people to whom a great debt of gratitude is owed:

Robert Atkinson, Captain G.P.D. Hall RN, Donald MacDonald, James MacGeoch, William Matheson, Kenneth Paterson.

The staff of: the Scottish Record Office; the Manuscript Departments of the National Library of Scotland and Edinburgh University Library; Hydrographic Survey Records, Admiralty, Taunton; Stornoway Gazette; Stornoway Public Library; Comunn Eachdraidh Nis.

From Ness: Angus Campbell (Am Puilean, Swainbost), Norman Campbell (Knockaird), Allan MacDonald (Stugan, Cross), Calum MacDonald (Eorodale), Iain Gordon MacDonald and Norma MacDonald (Habost), Murdo and Mary MacFarlane (Port of Ness), Mrs Dolina MacIver (Habost), Norman MacKay (Tormod Beag, Skigersta), Finlay MacKenzie (Habost), John and Peggy MacKenzie (Swainbost Farm), Donald MacLeod (Baile Glom), Donald MacLeod

(Port of Ness), Donald MacLeod (North Dell), Harriet MacLeod (Edgemoor Square), John MacLeod (Port of Ness), Mrs Seonag MacLeod (North Dell), William MacLeod (P.O. Cross), William MacLeod (Cross), Annie MacSween (North Dell), Mrs D. Morrison (Fivepenny), Donald Morrison (Knockaird), Rev. Jack Morrison, Mrs Margaret Morrison (Port of Ness), John Murray (Snagaidh, North Dell), Angus Murray (Skigersta), Mrs Murray (Lionel), Christina Smith (South Dell), Norman Smith (Habost), Mrs Jean Weir (Swainbost);

and Rev. Stanley Bennie (Stornoway), Bill Lawson (Northton), Rev. Donald Macaulay (Bernera), Finlay MacLeod (Shawbost), John Murdo MacLeod (Stornoway), Norman MacLeod (Stornoway), Alex Murdo Morrison (Barvas), Ann Sutherland (Uig).

CONTENTS

Tobha Ronaidh and Geodha Meadhar from Fianuis.

(photo. Robert Atkinson)

RONA

From the highest point of Rona, the Tòbha, you can see the hills of Lewis and the mountains of Sutherland when the weather is clear, though they are over forty miles away. More often there is nothing to be seen but a mist, which blurs the meeting of sky and sea and lies between the grey clouds and the white-flecked swelling ocean. If you are sailing to Rona in a small boat there will be many hours when you are out of sight of land. The island is so small and far off that those who live nearest to it, in Kinlochbervie or in Ness, rarely or never catch a glimpse, even on the best of days. But when the wind is, say, northeast and the sky is overcast, it is sometimes possible to make out the Tòbha from the top of Beinn Dail in Ness and from one of the smaller peaks near Cape Wrath, a tantalising sight indeed to anyone who would like to be ashore on Rona.

At a time older than history and unrecorded even in tradition, Rona came to be considered part of Ness, the northern district of Lewis. How this was confirmed is told in a story which was written down by Mrs Macleod, Ocean Villa, Port of Ness, in November 1885. Clearly the seafaring men of Ness and of Sutherland knew that the island lay an equal distance away from each of them.

> "It was disputed at one time whether the Island of Rona belonged to the mainland or to the Lewis. The matter was settled in this way. It was agreed that a boat should start from the mainland and another from Ness at the same hour, each boat manned with six men, and that they should pull or row to the Island of Rona. The first party who was successful in putting a peat fire on the Island, the Island would be given over to their proprietor. As the Ness boat neared Rona, they were chagrined to find the mainland boat a good many paces ahead of them. The Ness men pulled with all their strength, when a happy thought struck one of their crew more thoughtful than his fellows. He jumped from his seat and snatching a live peat from the fire they had in the boat he threw the peat on to the Island, thus securing it to the Proprietor of the Lewis."[1]

In 1866 the Reverend Malcolm MacPhail heard the same story in Ness at North Dell, although he was told that the Ness team was composed of Morrisons, and that one of them stood up in the boat and shot a burning arrow onto the island, setting the dry grass on fire. It was even said that it was the mainland boat that threw the peat, and that a Morrison cut off his own hand, or just a finger, and cast it ashore to lay a claim that was stronger for being in blood.[2] Alexander Carmichael, who was in Ness at much the same time as MacPhail, heard that the contest had been between the MacLeods of Lewis and the MacKays of Reay, who had set off in sixteen-oared galleys each manned by twenty one men, and that one of the Macleods had cut off his arm.[3] Such a tale also lies behind the ancient ownership of St. Kilda.

In any event, Rona was part of Ness, and to the people of that district the island has always been known as "Ronaidh" or "Ronaidh an t'haf", Rona of the Ocean. This latter name appears in 1561 as "Rona na nav";[4] and about 1700 a boat crew was wrecked on "Rona-a-taiff".[5] It was in this way that an old man on Raasay some years ago distinguished between sheltered Rona at the north end of his island and Rona far out in the wild Atlantic. A third Rona lies on the east side of Benbecula. They have little in common, these three islands, except that they were all once inhabited, and are all rocky and bare enough to have deserved the Viking name of "hraun-ey", rough island. Some think that "Rona" might derive from the Gaelic "ron", a seal, or from a holy man called Ronan. Surveyors of the 1850s who found it confusing that three islands should share one name used the description "North", which has since remained on most maps and charts.[6]

What can be said of such a tiny, remote isle, often hidden away in storms? It might be thought that any story of the place would not be worth the telling. Yet deserted, desolate Rona plays a part in the lives of Ness people today; fishermen know it, children hear of it and there are tales told of it — some with their origins in a time before the island had a name. There is much indeed to be told, and much still to be discovered, about Rona, with its lonely cliffs and its quiet green slopes.

PART 1

AN OLDER WORLD

The Holy Man and the Island

When Mr MacPhail went to North Dell in 1866 he met there an old man called Angus Gunn. With the words of a visitor he described Angus as "the noted Ness traditionalist",[7] a poor phrase that really means that he had met one of the last great storytellers, a treasure-house of history and legend, who carried in his memory an unmatched knowledge of Ness, its places and its past. Roderick Campbell, author of "The Father of St. Kilda", remembered how, as a boy, he had learned much lore from "old Angus Gunn . . . who told his tales of old with much emotion, tears glittering on his long white eye-lashes, and running down his aged cheeks."[8] To have questioned the truth of what Angus said would have been insulting. "He had a rare, a marvellous and uncontaminated memory; and truth telling, literal, strict and absolute, was the first article of his faith". Mr Campbell sailed past Rona one bright morning in July 1859, when the sea sparkled in the sun, and he thought of all he had learned — "Many a tale of this island I had drunk in almost with my mother's milk. Old Angus Gunn was full of its traditions".[9] No wonder that he was, for Angus had lived on the island himself.

It is likely that, when he was at Dell, Mr MacPhail visited William Watson, who had also drawn upon Angus Gunn's wealth of know-ledge. Like Campbell and Watson, Malcolm MacPhail sensed the unusual quality of the storyteller, and noted that "Rona and Angus are by the law of association inseparably united in my memory". The folklorist Alexander Carmichael felt this way too. He took down from Angus a story about Rona which made him feel as if he had glimpsed the very root of the Ness world.[10]

The story which Angus Gunn told, and in which he lives on, belongs to that region in which legend and history meet and become confused. It resembles the story of St. Patrick's arrival in Ireland, or that of Jonah, and survives best in a version composed by Carmichael from Angus Gunn's own words.

"A man came to Ness", Angus Gunn began, "in the dark grey dawn of the ages long ago". He was a good, holy man, and he built himself a chapel or prayer house, "tigh ùrnuigh", at Rudh' Eoropaidh, within hearing of the sea; and the birds, the animals and the seals were his companions. The chapel, built above the village of Fivepenny, was at some time called Teampull Rònain or Ronaidh, and the site is today a green mound with a few stones and a fence across it.

Living on the outer edge of habitable land, the holy man found that the people disregarded his teaching and pursued ways of wickedness. In particular, he found it difficult to put up with the disputes of quarrelsome women which seemed to go on within his hearing. For these reasons he resolved to leave the district, and he prayed to be delivered, not caring where else he might go. In the darkness of his cell he heard a voice responding to his prayer, telling him what he must do. He must rise up and go to the landing place at Cunndal, the bay west of Eoropie, and there he would find a ferry boat, a "messenger" to carry him away. "Eirich! Eirich! Tha an t-each iomchair air an laimrig". Whether it was to Cunndal or to Stoth that he had to go, the holy man did not obey at first, but after the voice had called three times he rose and made his way through the night to the shore.

When he came to the landing place he found his "ferryboat" stretched out along the rock, waiting. It appeared as a great black shape there, and was said by Angus Gunn to be the "cionaran-crò", indescribable but not least among the creatures haunting the depths of the sea. A rhyme taken down about 1860 from Kenneth Morrison, cottar in Skye, places these creatures in their order:

> Seachd sgadain,
> Sàth bradain;
> Seachd bradain,
> Sàth ròin;
> Seachd ròin,
> Sàth muc-mhara bheag;
> Seachd muca-mara beag,
> Sàth muc-mhara mhòr;
> Seachd muca-mara mòr,
> Sàth cionarain-crò;
> Seachd cionarain-crò
> Sàth mial mhòr a' chuain.

> Seven herrings
> Feast for a salmon;
> Seven salmon
> Feast for a seal;
> Seven seals
> Feast for a small whale;
> Seven small whales
> Feast for a great whale;
> Seven great whales
> Feast for a "cionaran-crò";
> Seven "cionarain-crò"
> Feast for the great beast of the ocean[11]

After they had looked at each other the holy man climbed upon the creature's back where he stood or sat while it slowly moved out to the open sea.

The "cionaran-crò" took its burden safely across rough wintery miles of surging waters to the uninhabited island now called Rona. When the holy man leaped ashore at last on the storm-beaten headland of "Sròn an Tintinn", his sacred presence drove back the strange beasts that were there — as Angus Gunn seems to have described them, dog-like creatures with sharp claws and serpents with fangs. They retreated until they slid off down the sloping rocks of the island's southern shore at a place afterwards known as Leac na Sgròb, the scratched slab, where the deep narrow grooves made by the slithering claws can yet be seen, in particular at the western end of Leac na Sgròb, where they are called Scròbagan nam Biast, the scratches of the beasts. "In strong gales", as another visitor was told, "the sea beats against these rocks with great violence".

The holy man has been named in tradition as Ronan. He was undoubtedly a monk of the early Celtic Christian Church, one of St. Columba's kind, and it seems that, like many of his fellow churchmen in Ireland, he sought what the monks called "a desert place in the sea". Cormac, for instance, sailed north in a coracle "for fourteen summer days and as many nights" and survived an attack by loathsome sea creatures, in search of a suitable "hermitage" on a lonely island where he might live and pray in peaceful isolation.[12] Off the northeast coast of England, Cuthbert retreated to the Farnes. "The Farne", wrote his biographer, "is an island far out to sea . . . cut off on the landward side by very deep water and facing, on the other side, out towards the limitless ocean. The island was haunted by devils; Cuthbert was the first man brave enough to live there alone. At the entry of our soldier of Christ . . . the devil fled and his host of allies with him".[13] So Ronan was not alone in exiling himself to an ocean wilderness, from which the wickedness was expelled by the holy presence.

According to Angus Gunn, Ronan had a half brother, Flannan, who went to the islands west of Loch Roag, and two sisters called Brianuil and Mionagan or Miriceal, who followed him to Rona. Angus never knew how they got there. There was a story that Brianuil went out with her brother on the back of the "cionaran-crò", but that may be merely to explain how she managed to be on the island with him. For some time, perhaps years, they lived quietly there together, until one day when Ronan and Brianuil were down on Fianuis, the northern headland of Rona. As they were climbing back up the slope, Leathad Fhianuis, Ronan looked up and saw his sister ahead of him. "My dear sister, it is yourself that is handsome", he said. "What beautiful legs you have". Her reply was brief: "It is time for me to

1936. Eastwards along the south coast of Rona to Slochd a Phriosan and Hellair, with the sloping rocks of Leac na Sgròb where the creatures of the island slid off before the advancing footsteps of the holy man.

(photo Robert Atkinson)

5

leave the island". Somehow she reached Sula Sgeir, the rock of the gannets, ten miles away to the west, where she died after several years of windswept solitude. On Rona, Ronan built two chapels or cells, one for himself, the other for his remaining sister and called after her Teampull Mhionagain or Teampull Mhiriceil. Upon his death the holy man was buried near his cell, and over his grave was set a stone carved in the rough shape of a cross, though who dug the grave and raised the stone is not told.

Such was the tale heard from Angus Gunn by Watson, Carmichael and MacPhail about 1866. "When asked", wrote MacPhail, "if he believed this story Angus replied that the good men of old now dust told him so and why should he doubt them". Angus was a lonely survival, "a peak of a submerged world", observing the ancient rocks and the starry heavens and living in the heroic Fingalian times of his stories. "Now", Mr MacPhail said regretfully in 1897, "the waters of oblivion have covered this very remarkable man".[14]

The Chapels of Rona

Like Angus Gunn, the Rona chapels were themselves a reminder to later generations of a mysterious past. Around them gathered ancient traditions and a thousand years after Ronan and his sisters walked the grassy slopes of the island the holy man's prayerhouse was still the scene of rituals that belong to some remote time.

"Within this Ile", wrote Donald Monro in 1549, "thair is ane chapell callit St. Ronans Chapell, into the quhilk chapell (as the ancients of that cuntrie alledgis) thay use to leave ane spaid and ane schoole (i.e. shovel) quhan ony deid, and upon the morn findis the place of the grave taiknit with ane spaid (as thai alledge)".[15] The "ancients" or old people of Rona spoke mostly of Ronan, and did not mention Teampull Mhionagain, although about 1680 John Morison, a tacksman of Bragar and member of the Brieve family, wrote that "In this Ronay there are tuo little cheapels where Sanct Ronan lived all his tym as ane heremite".[16] Morison's two chapels were probably separate buildings, but this is not certain, as by his time St. Ronan's cell had been extended to the west with the addition of a larger room, said to date from about the 12th century. The spade and the shovel may even have been left in this new part, which, being spacious, could serve a congregation of islanders much better than the small cell intended for the devotions of only one or two inhabitants.

In the Middle Ages Rona was included within the Bishopric of the Isles, and it was a long time before the effects of the Reformation were felt in this far-flung outpost. In 1561 a rental of the "Bischopis landis within the Illis" named "Rona na nav",[17] and Thomas Knox, Bishop

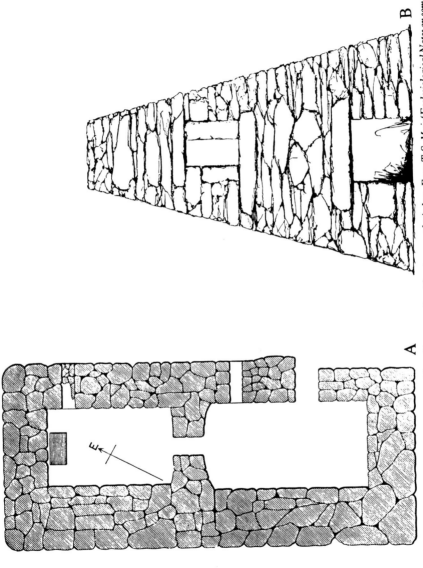

A The chapel and cell (top) in Rona. B The interior of the cell's west wall, with entrance and window. From T.S. Muir 'Ecclesiological Notes on some of the Islands of Scotland' p. 92 and p. 93.

7

of the Isles, concerned himself in 1626 with "The North Ilandis lyand betwix the row (point) of Ardmarochie and the Ile of Rona beyond the Lewis . . ."[18] Catholicism of a kind persisted among the Rona people, chiefly because of their isolation, and with it the customs and traditions adhering to the old faith. Thus in his account of the island in the late 17th century MacKenzie referred to long-established religious practices:

> "There is a chappel in the midst of the Isle, where they meet twice or thrice a day. One of the families is hereditary Bedell and the Master of that stands at the Altar and prayeth; the rest kneel upon their knees, and joyn with him. Their Religion is the Romish Religion".[19]

It was therefore a meeting of two worlds when the Protestant minister of Barvas, Donald Morison, went out to visit the Catholic islanders in the 1680s. Some forty years earlier Morison was described as "minister of the Kirk of Ness in Lews" and then as "preacher at the Kirk of Stornuay".[20] At this time Ness had become officially part of Barvas parish, to which Morison had returned as minister by 1684 and where he still was at the end of 1695. The Ness townland of Habost was set aside as a glebe for him, and according to Martin Martin the island of Rona was considered part of that glebe. It was probably for this reason that Morison made an expedition to Rona, where there were people who may have heard of him and perhaps held him in reverence but who undoubtedly went their separate ways as far as religious practice was concerned. The minister was deeply impressed by his experience on Rona, and he gave a full account to Martin a few years later.[21]

When he arrived in the island, probably on a summer day with the sea calm, "the natives" flocked around him in a friendly way and greeted him as an expected visitor:

> "God save you, pilgrim, you are heartily welcome here; for we have had repeated apparitions of your person among us . . . and we heartily congratulate your arrival in this our remote country".

Perhaps it was the leading religious figure, the "beadle", who spoke. Then an islander wished to show his respect by walking round Morison "sunways" and blessing him, but the latter requested him not to do so. To the mind of the minister, as to visitors of more recent times, such rituals had none of their original significance and might seem mere superstition. Yet "this poor man was not a little disappointed, as were also his neighbours; for they doubted not but this ancient ceremony would have been very acceptable to me". One of them said that they owed as much to Morison as "their chief and patron".

After these uncertain moments the little group moved up the slope to the houses, and there Morison saw "a chapel dedicated to St.

Ronan, fenced with a stone-wall round it". He found it neatly cared for, as the people swept it clean each day, and on the altar lay a wooden plank about ten feet long: "every foot has a hole in it, and in every hole a stone, to which the natives ascribe several virtues . . ." One of the stones was particularly effective in "promoting speedy delivery to a woman in travail". The minister also learned that every Sunday morning the people assembled in the chapel and repeated the Lord's Prayer, the Creed, and the Ten Commandments, a custom that at least in part may have won rather more approval from him. Little did Morison know, as he walked about in the course of duty, that these hospitable parishioners would soon be no more.

It seems quite possible, however, that another unusual visitor came to Rona before it lost its native inhabitants. The story begins with the Morisons of Bragar. John Morison's eldest son was Roderick, known later in life as the Blind Harper, An Clàrsair Dall. Among his compositions were verses on the subject of a priest whose behaviour was considered disgraceful for one of his calling, and though the work is not dated it must relate to a certain Catholic priest called Cornelius Con, who was in Lewis about 1690.[22] At that time there was one Catholic family known in Lewis, that of George Mackenzie of Kildun, who was said to have been blind like the Harper. Kildun was near Dingwall, but Mackenzie resided at Aignish, east of Stornoway, and was tacksman of lands in the Point district granted to him by his brother Kenneth, third Earl of Seaforth, who died in 1678. About 1688 two priests came to Mackenzie's house; one was Patrick O'Car-olan, who did not stay for long, and the other was Cornelius Con, who lived at Aignish as chaplain and tutor in the household. Con may have been the priest from whom, according to Martin, some opportunist fishermen requested aid in improving their catch:

"I was told that about 14 years ago, three or four fishermen who then forsook the Protestant communion, and embraced the Romish faith, having the opportunity of a Popish priest on the place, they applied themselves to him for some of the holy water; it being usual for the priests to sprinkle it into the bays, as an infallible means to procure plenty of herring, as also to bring them into those nets that are besprinkled with it. These fishers accordingly having got the water, poured it upon their nets before they dropped them into the sea; they likewise turned the inside of their coats outwards, after which they set their nets in the evening at the usual hour. The Protestant fishers, who used no other means than throwing their nets into the sea, at the same time were unconcerned; but the Papists being impatient and full of expectation, got next morning betimes to draw their nets, and being come to the place, they soon perceived that all their nets were lost; but the Protestants found their nets safe, and full of herring: which was no small mortification to the priest and his proselytes, and exposed them to the derision of their neighbours".[23]

9

So, at least, went the story, and the neighbours soon had something else to joke about at the priest's expense.[24] Mackenzie of Kildun had three sons and several daughters:

"He was a Baptist [i.e. a Papist] and got a priest to his house at Aignish to teach his children. This priest they called Mr Conn who became so very familiar in the Laird's family as to throw off the Sacerdotal restraint by getting one of the Laird's daughters with child — The Laird discovering this abuse in conjunction with his friends punished Mr Conn by confinement in desolate Islands about the Lewis coast — till at last he escaped going through much suffering from cold and hunger".

Among those who found the episode amusing was the Reverend Angus Morison at Contin, who remarked in a letter that "Kildins daughter Jean is wt childe and as the report goes she has declair'd to some friends, priest Conn is the man ha ha". There were many, however, including the outraged father and possibly the Blind Harper, to whom Con's misdemeanour deserved the kind of punishment meted out. He was first of all ordered away to the island of Flodda at the mouth of Loch Roag, where he was living in 1694, under the custody of a MacLennan, one of the sons of Iain mac Ruaidhri Chlèirich, tacksman of Little Bernera; and it was this guardian who removed him to a still more lonely hiding place when the Privy Council had got wind of his presence on Flodda. The Council sent an officer called Lieutenant Walkingshaw to investigate, but when he landed on Flodda he found no trace of the prisoner. All that he saw to interest him was a partly-effaced message scrawled on the shoulder blade of a sheep, the words being sufficient to show that MacLennan had reached the island first. In fact Con had been taken to Rona and was still kept there in 1696. It is not certain whether the native population was still on Rona then; if it was not, then Con had a truly lonely time.

The affair of Cornelius Con, sometimes called O'Con ("Ockon"), was still concerning members of the Privy Council in 1697, by which time Kildun's nephew, then Earl of Seaforth, was being blamed for the notoriously brutal treatment meted out to the "priest". There was correspondence in high political places on the subject. On 23rd September 1697 Sir James Ogilvie wrote to the Earl of Marchmont, urging further action over Con:

"What usage he hes mett with is noture [i.e. well-known], and tho you have no legal proofe that it was done by the Earle of Seaforth's order, yet you have what is convinceing, for the barbaritie has been committed within my Lords lands, and none durst use such practices ther without his order; and the cause of al is weal knowen, his turning Protestant and marrying ane relation of my lords. Therfor in justice my lord ought to be imprisoned if he doe not present him".[25]

It is interesting to find that Con had actually changed his religion and married Jean, events confirmed in a further letter, this time from the Lord Advocate to the Earl of Tullibardine, dated 21st October 1697. The whole episode was summarised, on the basis of information received:

"The storie of Cornelius Con is thus. The man was a preist, and falls in love with Kildeins dauchter, and is accepted. Kildein, Earl Seaforth's uncle, is a papist, and condemnes the intrigue as both base and irreligious. Cornelius quits his religion, and caries away his mistress, and maries her, but is, shortly thereafter, seased and imprisoned, and his keeping with all severity committed to one McClellan, by Earl Seaforth, who, as its said, gives McClellan £100 scots yearly for his paines. What hardships Cornelius suffered at first I cannot be particular in, but after his being removed from island to island, when Lieut. Walkingshaw was last sent by the Councells order, he found he had bein keept in a bare rock in the sea [i.e. Flodda] where no house [was], but that Cornelius had three places of shelter against the weather that by walking and lyeing he had paved to a smoothness, and that McClellan, who lives in an island about two miles distant, sent him in provisions once in the sax weakes or once a quarter, but McClellan getting notice of the coming of the partie, by a boat that went from the main island before the Lieut. could stay her, had, tuo dayes befor, carried Cornelius away so that all the Lieut. found was Cornelius sheltering places, and in one of them in the clift of the rock the shoulder bone of a sheep with these words written on it, Doctor Cornelius Con caried away such a day, and, on the other side, his imploring King Williams justice, with some broken words, the rain having effaced the rest, as if directing to find him out by Stornway. This bone is in the clerk of councels hand. Kildein, tho' blind, fled, but wrot a letter to the Lieut. complaining of the wrong Cornelius had done him, but purging himself of violence or revenge, and plainly eneugh insinuating that Earl Seaforth was his persequuter. Withall, he said, his daughter had left Cornelius and hated him more than ever she loved him. This is the sume of what was informed . . ."[26]

A week after this letter, the Earl of Tullibardine heard from Patrick Murray of Dollary, who commented on the "great crymes and ryots" committed by the Earl of Seaforth, and especially on how "He caused cary a priest, who hade disobleidged him, to ane island, and keept him ther all alone, without fyre or cloathes, these seaven yeares past, only he sent him some meall to keep in his lyfe". Murray added that the Privy Council had ordered Seaforth to produce the man, and that on receiving notice of this order Seaforth had taken precautionary steps — "it is said that the man is now murdered".[27]

Since "These things concern both the justice and honour of the Government", Tullibardine did what he could to ensure "that that business of O'Cons be effectually prosecuted and that my Lord Seaforth be brought to answer for it".[28] It turned out, however, that

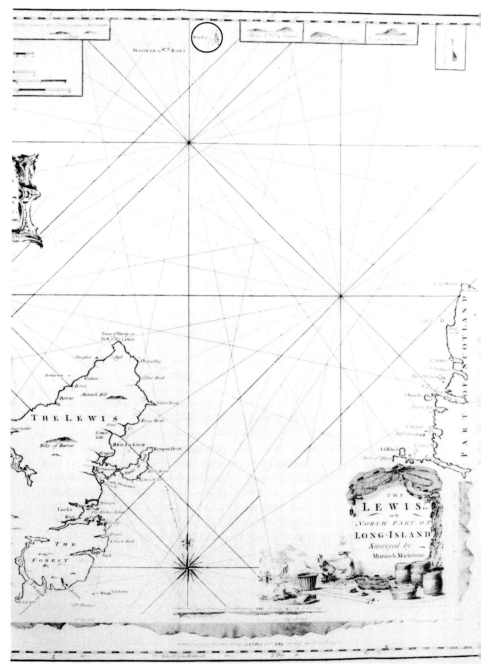

Murdo Mackenzie's chart Orcades *showing the island of Rona in relation to the island of Lewis and Sutherland.*
(photo. Finlay Macleod)

Con had not been murdered, for nearly a year later, in early September 1698, he had evidently been rescued from his island captivity and had gone to Edinburgh to plead his case. There he was put in prison in the Castle, from which he himself wrote letters seeking his freedom. On 22nd December 1698 he wrote to the Lord Chancellor:

"My Lord, I am these fifteen weeks close prisonour incapable to write to my countrey or friends for a supply, daily running in debt heare and not able to pay it, as I have signifyed in my petition to the Lords of the Treasury and has yett got noe answear or precept".

He wished a hearing so that he might learn the accusations against him:

"I have been euermore dutifull to Gouerment which occationed my sufferings amongst wilde vnruly persons, and though I am a stranger in Scotland, yet am a loyal and real subject to the King of Brittaine and therfore expects justice. I came of my free accord to give the Gouerment an account of my sufferings and of my persecutor against whome I libled on a bone, and did expect better encouragement then imprisonment".[29]

Con asked for his liberty, but was still in the Castle on 18th January 1699 when he wrote again, complaining of the extremity to which he was then reduced and wishing to know what his offence was. By 4th May 1699 he was still under some restraint but had a greater measure of freedom and was hoping he would be granted a certificate of his sufferings for the Protestant cause: "this castle is a poor place for a weak purse, yet is a paradise to me in respect of the Papisticall Purgatory the eight years. I question if the Pope will so soon get out of his purgatory if he goes there".[30] Within a short while Con was completely free and thankful for his survival as well as his release.

The thread of ancient religion was broken when about 1700 Rona was for a short while deserted. Then the arrival of different people coming out from Lewis with a fund of inherited knowledge about the island restored life around the chapel and cell of St. Ronan. It is certainly true that St. Ronan's cell continued to be regarded as a sacred place, but nothing was recorded of Teampull Mhionagain, and it seems that the buildings themselves began to decay. The new island population usually amounted to no more than one family and a single family needed only its own fireside for a place of worship, so that there was little reason, other than curiosity, to enter the chapel. For rare, important occasions, a visit to Lewis was necessary, and early in the 19th century MacCulloch discovered that although the occupant at the time was contented enough he did long for a chance to have his two children christened: "for this purpose he had resolved to visit Lewis when his period of residence was expired".[31]

In spite of the marked break with the past, the cell was maintained in some sort of order, and rituals and beliefs continued to be part of Rona life. It is possible, even likely, that these stemmed from the distant past, handed on in the villages of Ness where Rona had always been familiar, even among those who had never been there, and perhaps the ritual of the three-holed gravestone was of this kind. It was described by Iain MacKay to T.S. Muir about 1857, after the latter had made a drawing of the stone:

'And the cross?' inquired Iain.
'I saw three or four crosses, though only one that was whole — a rough weather-worn stumpy thing, standing some two or three feet high, in the middle of the burying ground'.
'With three holes bored through, — you saw it?'
'To be sure; look, there it is: do you know anything about it?'
'There was something — if I could mind it — that the big folks used to talk of, — something about the holes. The night before the New Year, they came to look through them, after they had put the candles on the altar'.
'On the altar in the teampull, do you mean? What did you put candles there for?'
'I do not know: we always did it: it was the custom: we put two, — one at the one end and one at the other, and then went outside to see the light coming through the door and the window over it: and after that we went to the cross; — but I cannot well remember; — it is a long time ago . . .'[32]

MacKay's people looked at the candle-light glowing from inside that lonely cell, no longer knowing why they did so. And there were the mysterious three holes in a short stone cross, and a supposed "Teampull nam Manach" also. In a letter to Muir Daniel Murray, tenant of Rona at the time, made remarks on Angus Gunn, whose tale of the holy man's journey to the island on the sea creature was followed with information on this second chapel:

"It was this Ronan that built the east end of the present teampull, or the part that still stands of it. After him, Roman Catholics occupied the island, and they built another teampull which was called *Teampull nam Manach*. It was outside the grave-yard, and about 15 yards from the east end of the present teampull; it was roofed with timber and thatched with straw, and was about the size of the west end of the present temple, with an altar in the middle 4 feet square by 3 feet high, and having a round gray stone on the top. The roof and part of the wall was pulled down four hundred years since, but the altar and part of the wall (3 feet in height) were standing when Angus Gunn was on the island . . ."[33]

The "Teampull nam Manach", chapel of the monks, might have been the same as Teampull Mhionagain, and the round gray stone one of those seen by Reverend Morison on his visit towards the end of the 17th century. As it is, in all these vague memories and more exact

14

Rona from the South East.
From Harvey Brown & T.E. Buckley. 'A Vertebrate Fauna of the Outer Hebrides' Edinburgh 1888
opp. p. xxxvi.

traditions the old Rona can be felt, withdrawn, changed, disappearing over time's horizon.

Muir was eager to ransack Iain MacKay's store of recollections. "Turn out another mouthful", he said, "and try if you can remember more. Was there anything about the teampull, then, that is not to be seen now . . .?" By "teampull" he meant St Ronan's cell. "I missed nothing — in the teampull, I mean," Iain dutifully replied, "but a wooden pin, turned up like a hook, that Saint Ronan hung his hat upon, when he went in. Before I left the island, you could see it sticking out of the wall at the side of the door, after you were through it and on your legs again. I remember it quite well: we used to hang things upon it — we children, I mean, for the older folks did not go in so often, the door was such a hinder — any little thing we had with us — a wool-waif, or the like, — we hung it upon the pin, to see if it would be still there when we came back next time". It had been Iain's first task, on revisiting the island, to see if the pin was present, and he had crawled into the cell, only to find that it was gone.

Muir was interested to know whether the cell had altered since Iain's childhood, and whether much of it had tumbled down. Though it seemed dilapidated on the outside, the building was, Iain said, as perfect as ever within — "just the same as ever it was". Muir asked him whether the exterior stonework had collapsed because the people had taken out stones from time to time to repair their house.

"No, we never did that. Not one of us, I am sure, would have touched a stone in teampull Rona, or in anything near it, or in the *cladh* [i.e. burial ground]: we did not like to meddle with anything there. The wind sometimes blew down bits of the wall round the place, but we always put them up again, and laid turf on the top. We laid turf also on the top of the chapel, and put lime made from shells among the stones, to keep them

15

together; for we thought a great deal of the teampull, and would not have liked it to fall down".

Switching the conversation briefly from cell to chapel, Muir said he had seen lime on the cell walls but none of those of the other building. Iain agreed, for his family had shown little regard for the broken-down later part and had carried out no repairs. Muir told his guide that the extension was much like ruins he had seen in many parts of Lewis, whereas the cell with its converging walls was quite different. What had the cell roof been like, he wondered.

> ". . . I think the roof, if I mind right, bowed over like that we have on our black houses, only it was made of stones, but many of them being away, we used to mend it with turf — great big ones, which we heaped, here and there, where the broken places were, up over the flat stones that lie across from wall to wall in the inside . . . I mind we were often on the top of it putting on turfs; for the wind was always blowing them off in the winter time . . ."

Though Iain had been careful to maintain the roof, he and others who had lived on the island were not so worried about the cell doorway, which was so silted up with earth that Iain was compelled "to draggle myself forward, lying full-length on the ground", to get in. When the surveyors arrived in 1850 they did not apparently think much of this style of entry. "I did not like to believe it", Iain told Muir gently,

> "but I was told that the Sappers, when on the island measuring it, or doing something or other there . . . made a hole in the teampull, at one end of it, just between the roof and the wall; and I did see that stones had been taken out of it there, as I was looking round it, and you drawing inside at the time. May be you don't believe it; but some of the Ness men, who were over to clip the sheep, told me they saw them do it, because they wanted to know what sort of place it was inside, but couldn't make up their minds to the trouble of going in by the door".

Muir was shocked at this, and wondered if Sir James Matheson, the owner, had received any word of the outrage. "I fancy not: the place is so far away, many things may be done there, and he . . .". Sir James was undoubtedly too busy to listen to such reports. Muir declared that Sir James would have to be told and that he would have to instruct the tenant on his next visit to the island to repair the hole and patch up loose parts of the wall with lime and sods.[34] However the gap had been caused, it proved to be many years before the damage was made good.[35]

With the departure of the last family from Rona about 1840 Teampull Ronan, the chapel, the graveyard, as well as all the other places with sacred associations, became mere relics, objects of anti-

1936. The holy man's cell with its broken roof, and the chapel to the right.

(photo. Robert Atkinson)

17

The cell with its roof repaired and the adjoining chapel 1966.

quarian and historical attention. Visitors, whether surveyors or naturalists or yachtsmen, wrote notes which are a mixture of cold fact and guesswork:

> "There are a graveyard and Church . . . attached to the village. The former is enclosed by a wall composed of Stone and Earth and contains in or about its centre a rude stone cross without any inscription. The latter is on the south side of the former and is about 7 yards long by 4 yards wide. The walls are still standing and are about 6 feet high, and composed of stone and lime. There is a small house at its S. East end, which appears to have been formerly used as a vestry as it communicates with the Church by means of a small door or opening. Its walls are built of lime and stone and roofed with the same materials. It is about 6 feet long, four feet wide and about 8 feet high. It is plastered and whitewashed with lime on the inside which Keeps it dry and prevents it from being in ruins like the others".[36]

Year by year the atmosphere of creed and candles slipped away from Rona, and there are fewer people in Ness who can look back through the many centuries to the days of St. Ronan and his cell. In most summers now, four fulmars nest in Teampull Ronan, one in each corner. To enter by the low door in the western gable wall you have to crawl in on hands and knees, much as Iain MacKay did, and immediately the fulmars fire their oil from left and right as your head comes in view. Once in, it is possible to avoid the efforts of all of them by standing at the very centre of the cell. Against the eastern wall is the little stone altar, but otherwise the room is bare, with a floor of earth and jumbled stone and walls that lean towards each other, the narrow space between them at the top bridged with five stone slabs. In the southern wall is a recess about one foot square, and a wooden peg with a hole through it juts from the stonework above the altar. The only window is the small one over the door, which lets in little light. In such an austere and silent place decoration would seem unsuitable, but the faces of the walls as well as the altar have been covered with a mortar of shell-lime and clay which here and there shows what could be artificial whirls and rings. This is the cell, that is the altar, where the holy man of long ago worshipped, with the wind and sea beating around the narrow silent spot; and today the walls, no longer protected with annual repairs of turf, house only the starlings and the fork-tailed petrels.

A young fulmar beside the altar in the cell.   *(photo. Author's Collection)*

19

The three-holed stone which stood so long in the midst of the graveyard is no longer on the island. More than fifty years ago it was taken to Ness and placed in Teampull Mholuaidh at Eoropie. Though cracked into two parts it is still complete, with one pale, whitish face, which perhaps lay upon the ground at some time, and a more weathered side. If light is allowed to shine across this dark surface it picks out what neither T.S. Muir nor any other visitor ever remarked upon, the figure of a man outlined with a groove, the three holes passing by chance under the armpits and through the throat, and also distinctive the exaggerated male organs signifying fertility. The cross-shaped stone, with its human figure and its mysterious three holes, may date from the sixth or seventh century, and may have been, as it used to be said, the stone that marked St. Ronan's grave.*

". . . that ancient race of people"

It is not known who the first inhabitants of Rona were, and St. Ronan stands, mysterious and alone with his sisters, in a dark, prehistoric world. The Vikings must have been on Rona. It is said that a Norse princess is buried there, her grave beside the walls of the chapel marked with a cross; and it is also told that the son of the King of Lochlann [Norway] lies in the island, buried without his head in a grave eighteen feet long.[37] John MacLeod, Iain Mhurdo, late boat-builder in Ness, said that the first people were "na papanaich", the Catholics, and that they had strange names, unlike any known in Ness. Of the relationships between the early Christian islanders and the Norsemen nothing is known.

There is an old Ness tradition that the race for Rona took the form of a dispute between local men and a party from 'Buchanhaven' on the mainland. The rivals met at Rona, and in the slaughter that followed all the mainlanders were killed. They were buried in the Rona graveyard, and the place is called Cnoc nam Bucanaich, the knoll of the Buchan men. It is perhaps of this strange event that another story is told, relating to Geodha nan Gall, the creek of the strangers. A Buchan boat went on the rocks of Rona, and when the crew came ashore they were given food by the islanders. Then suddenly the Rona people seized their guests and threw them down over the cliffs of Geodha nan Gall, which was named after them. Among the victims was a young lad, who, before meeting his end, cried out: "Will you not wait until I pick clean the bones!"

Whether or not the merciless fight with the Buchan sailors took

* A few years ago the stone disappeared from Ness but has now been returned, the two parts having been joined, and lies again in the Teampull at Eoropie.

place in the early days, it seems that the religious associations of the island were strong from the beginning, and that the first population was large and Christian. Some even said they were persecuted Christians. Angus Gunn remembered that in the graveyard were a great number of tombstones, some in the shape of a cross, or with a cross cut on them:

> "There were carved burial stones there too with swords and shields and crosses thereon; but they got broken and lost and most have disappeared".[38]

These stones were the last traces of a people long gone, and the undecorated few that remain, still standing in the ground or leaning against the wall inside the chapel, take their place beside other, small unmarked stones such as one might find in many an old Hebridean burial place. Among them, in Angus Gunn's time, was the "curious headstone" pierced with three holes but wrongly said to have on it "no carving or inscription of any sort".[39]

In 1549 Donald Monro, Archdeacon of the Isles, made his tour of the far-flung islands which composed the See. He then wrote his report, which included comments on the people living in Rona.[40] He said Rona, which he called "ane little Ile", was inhabited and cultivated by "simple people scant of ony Religion". Clearly they were not irreligious, but perhaps they did not in practice measure up to the Archdeacon's standards. The ground was dug with spades, and it grew abundant corn and abundant grass for stock to graze. The numbers of sheep and cattle were determined in accordance with the quality of the pasture by "thair awin auld rycht"; but so fertile was the island that the animals were numerous enough to keep the people in meat and pay the larger part of the rent. The barley meal they made was as fair and white as flour, and was placed inside the skins of sheep slain "belly flauchts", that is with the skin drawn off over the tail into the shape of a bag. This primitive method of flaying sheep was turned into a common Lewis phrase which is still known: "Feannadh a' bhuilg Ronach", the flaying of the Rona bag, a proverb used when, for example, someone has been "fleeced" in a lawsuit. The rent for Rona, which included dried mutton as well as meal and surplus stock and wild fowl, was sent not to the Bishop of the Isles but to MacLeod of Lewis, whose rights of possession no doubt strengthened with the approach of the Reformation.

The historian Buchanan, writing about 1580 and evidently making use of Monro's account, added some information of his own. He stated that the "master" of the island determined the number of families who might live there, and allowed them as many sheep and cattle as he thought sufficient for their needs. A surplus of produce was sent to the master in Lewis, and, "If ever they find they have too many people, they assign the extras as well to their master". Buchanan had formed a pleasing impression of the whole arrangement: "I think they are the only people in the whole world who lack nothing and have everything for their enjoyment. Equally ignorant of luxury and avarice, they have acquired from their ignorance of vices an innocence and peace of mind that others seek with great labour . . . The only thing that seems to fall short of the utmost felicity for them is that they do not realise the advantage of their condition."[41]

From such brief descriptions a picture of the early inhabitants of Rona begins to form. The cell, the chapel, and perhaps another chapel, stand amidst the small stones of the graveyard. Somewhere nearby are the houses, occupied by families whose number is fixed by a decision based on ancient custom and experience. The island is reckoned capable of supporting a limited quantity of stock; cornland of a size related to the pasture area needed for stock provides rich crops in good seasons; and the number of people is restricted in accordance with the restricted amount of produce. There are also other sources of food limited in a less direct way; valuable bird colonies occupy the cliffs and creeks, and both Monro and Buchanan record that the people of Rona catch many whales and other great fish of the ocean.

Fishing meant lines from the rocks and seaworthy boats. As the St. Kildans well knew, a boat had to be big enough to go upon the open sea and small enough to be hauled out above the reach of the greatest waves and swells. It is difficult to imagine how the whales were hunted, but that they were present in large numbers seems to be borne out by other evidence. Buchanan himself wrote of Lewis that

"in Ancient tymes so many Whales came in and were taken ther that by the report of old people, Twenty seeven some Great and some small hath been given as the Tithe to the Priests".[42]

Even in 1700 it was reported that "the Big Whales" still came round the Scottish coasts, especially in spring and autumn, and great must have been the excitement on Rona when a big whale was sighted.[43]

The actual population of the island in these times is not known, but somehow or other the idea got around that Rona was quite large and its inhabitants numerous. Buchanan wrote that it was "quite well populated", but late sixteenth century surveys concerned with the numbers capable of serving in the wars were more precise if not necessarily accurate. One report of 1593 included in its list: "Rona, perteining to McCloyd of the Lewes, LX men",[44] while another copy stated that "Rona may raise 50 men".[45] An anonymous description of the Isles written about the same time refers to "Ronalewis", associating it closely with the island of Lewis, and says that MacLeod, living at Stornoway Castle, "may raise on this part of the Ile callit Lewis 700 men with Rona, by [excluding] thame that labours the ground". More particularly it states that "Rona-Lewis is ane Ile of four mile lang perteining to McCloyd (of) Lewis, and it is 80 merk land. It payis 120 bolls victuall yeirlie, by [apart from] all uther customes and maillis. It is verie fertile of corns and store of gudes and quhyte fisches; but saltis na fisches, but eittis thair staiking and castis the rest on the land, and will raise 60 men".[46] Since this account is inaccurate regarding Rona's length it may also give an entirely mistaken number of men, and some sceptical reader has written against Rona in the document's margin "a monstruous lie". Skene, who published the description, noted that obviously there had been a confusion between Rona and the larger island of Bernera, but this may be doubted. Rona appears in Speed's atlas of 1599 and on other early maps rather too far to the east and south and often much larger than such islands as Eigg and Rum.

In 1598 confirmation was given to a contract whereby King James VI granted "The Ile of the lewis, Ronna lewis" and other parts to the group of noblemen called the "Gentilmen venturaris" of Fife who were supposed to take on this awkward area of the kingdom at their own risk. It had been difficult to make the inhabitants obey the King "be reasoun of the evill dispositioun and barbaritie of the peopill". The central government of the time certainly had little understanding or knowledge of Lewis society, and though the isles were reported as being rich "with ane incredibill fertilitie of cornis and store of fischeingis" and other commodities little could be made of these advantages because they were "possest be Inhabitantis qua ar voyd of ony knowledge of God or his Religioun" and who, "naturallie abhoiring all kynd of civilitie", had given themselves over to barbarity and inhumanity. The Fife gentleman were expected to sort the problem out.[47]

The plan miscarried and no such event took place. The MacLeods of Lewis, owners of Rona since long before the Reformation, must have known full well that this remote little part of their estate, for most of the time a law unto itself, could be left alone as long as it provided without protest its annual contribution of produce and an occasional surplus person.* Only a prejudiced and ignorant mind could have seen real or potential barbarity and inhumanity within its shores, and in any case few people of any kind knew anything at all about life on Rona. The maps and slight descriptions of the sixteenth century suggest that the island was thought to be far grander and more

---

* The Bishops of the Isles, even after the Reformation, considered Rona part of their possessions, and if there was rivalry between them and the MacLeods it may have helped to ensure that Rona was left to itself.

important than it really was, and clearly the government was out of touch. When the MacKenzies of Seaforth succeeded to the MacLeod possessions in the early 1600s nothing greatly changed. Over the mid seventeenth century George MacKenzie Earl of Seaforth was the remote mainland owner of Rona, the Shiant Islands, Great and Little Bernera and others in Loch Roag, the Flannan Islands and "lie twa Cunyngis-ilandis",[48] but had no acquaintance with any of them, and it would appear that the first possessor to take an interest was Sir George MacKenzie of Tarbat, who, with Sir Alexander MacKenzie of Coul and Colin MacKenzie of Redcastle, succeeded temporarily to the lands and barony of Lewis, including the castle of Stornoway and the several islands, in 1678.[49] Throughout this period long-established practices continued to prevail, so that even in 1680 or 1690 the old mediaeval world lingered on.

Between 1678 and 1688 John Morison, tacksman of Bragar, "a man who throws off verses with royal prodigality",[50] wrote his "Description of the Lewis", and he may well have been the source of the information sent in 1685 to Sir Robert Sibbald by Sir George Mac-Kenzie of Tarbat, who had it "from intelligent persons dwelling in the place".[51] Both agreed that Rona was customarily inhabited by five tenant families which, according to MacKenzie, "seldome exceed thirty souls in all", and that this had been the pattern for many generations. It was usual to have everything in common, or, as MacKenzie put it,

> "They have a kind of Commonwealth among them, in so far if any of them have more children than another, he that hath fewer taketh from the other what makes his num[b]er equal, and the excrescence of above thirty souls is sent with the Summer-boat to the Lewes to the Earle of Seafort their Master to [whom] they pay yearly some quantity of meal stitched up in sheep-skins and feathers of Sea-fowls . . .
>
> "There is alwayes one, who is Chief and commands the rest; and they are so well satisfied with their condition that they exceedingly bewail the condition of these as supernumerary they must send out of the Island".[52]

One wonders how the "supernumerary" people to be sent away were picked out. Perhaps it was a duty of the "Chief", a leading figure once to be found in most isolated Hebridean communities and one upon whom the task of difficult decision could be laid much as it was upon the skipper of a boat crew.

Then there were the seabirds, an aspect of Rona life upon which Morison had something to say. The wild fowls and their feathers, for home use and submitted as rent, could only be procured by skilled hunting on the cliffs or by approaching them in the dark as they slept:

> "The best of ther sustinance is fowll, which they take in girns, and

24

sometyms in a stormie night they creep to them, where they sleep thikest, and throwing some handfulls of sand over their heads as if it wer haile, they take them be the necks".[53]

The victims of the "girns" or snares probably included puffins and, perhaps, guillemots. It appears that there were no fulmars on Rona before the 1880s and that valuable source of food, feathers and lamp oil was not therefore available to the islanders as it was to the St. Kildans. Perhaps two or three hundred years ago the gannet bred on Rona as well as on Sula Sgeir where it is still found in abundance. At any rate Morison, like MacCulloch over a century later, speaks of this species as being used by the occupants of Rona:

> "Of the grease of these fowlls (especiallie the soline goose) they make ane excellent oyle called the *Gibanirtich*, which is exceeding good for healing of anie sore ore wound ore cancer either one man or beast; This I myselfe found true by experience, by applying it to the legg of a young gentleman which hade been inflamed and cankered for the space of tuo years; and his father being a trader south and north sought all Phisicians and Doctors with whom he hade occasione to meet, but all was in vaine; yet in three weeks tyme being in my hous was perfectlie whole be applying the foresaid oyle. The way they make it is they put the grease and fatt into the great gutt of the foull and so it is hung within a hous untill it run in oyle".[54]

Assuming the people on Rona indeed had boats from which they fished and caught whales, it was quite possible for them to make a "raid" upon Sula Sgeir and to bring back a haul of gannets young and old. The feathers, the fat, the meat, and the guts were all useful, and the necks could be turned into short-lived shoes, as was done in St. Kilda. Throughout the Hebrides seabird colonies were visited late in the breeding season by islanders who according to long-established custom had taken advantage of such a convenient and usually unfailing supply, and in doing so themselves the inhabitants of Rona merely observed generally accepted tradition.

The little kingdom of Rona was soon to welcome the Reverend Donald Morison on his visit to that detached fragment of his parish.[55] Perhaps he went there partly out of sheer curiosity or because he was intrigued by the Bragar tacksman's account; and whether he was met by the beadle or by the "king" of the island, who in any case might have been one and the same, he was immediately thrust into the heart of an ancient world, little changed over the centuries past. After the greetings he was conducted to "the little village where they dwell", before continuing to the chapel, and there he was as much impressed by what he found in the dwelling houses as he was by what he saw in the sacred buildings nearby.

Morison noticed the excellent barley, oats, cows and sheep for which the island was well known; but his attention was chiefly directed towards the people and their homes. There were the five families living a harmless life because they were perfectly ignorant of most of the world's many vices. They knew nothing of money, because they never sold or bought anything in their little "commonwealth", but their system of sharing did not extend to the cliffs, where, again like the St Kildans, "none of them will by any means allow his neighbour to fish within his property". They felt they had close links with the Ness people whose dress and language they shared, but were not much interested in the rest of the world and were amazed by such things as greyhounds, horses, and the huge population of Lewis. They seldom went anywhere, even to Ness, and preserved that independence which characterises a race that knows itself to be different. And the Reverend Morison still found that in a mysterious and unexplained way, "they take their surnames from the colour of the sky, rainbow and clouds".

The five families lived in three "inclosures". As Morison entered

A gull's eye view of the feannagan *or cultivation ridges around the settlement. The large curving wall almost encloses the graveyard, towards the left of which are the chapel and cell. Left of the cell again is the mound of a mysterious building, possibly Teampull Mhionagan, and beyond the graveyard are the three inclosures.*

(photo. Author's Collection)

26

each one of these he was greeted by the occupants, who took his hand and said, "Traveller, you are welcome here". Hospitable and kind to strangers, they received their visitor as if he had passed into another world, guiding him to the house assigned for his lodging, and, when he was seated on the bundle of straw which served as a chair, holding discourse with him for a little while, until they went off severally to their respective dwellings, where each family killed a sheep, flayed it in the old way, filled the skin with barley meal, and brought it back to the minister as a gift. "Traveller", their spokesman said, "we are very sensible of the favour you have done us in coming so far with a design to instruct us in our way to happiness, and at the same time to venture yourself on the great ocean; pray be pleased to accept of this small present, which we humbly offer as an expression of our sincere love to you". Morison accepted gratefully what was given with such good will, and his servant received "some pecks of meal" also; but the boat's crew, who had been in Rona before, were given only their board and lodging. So kindly was the manner in which these affairs were conducted that it now seems it was the Reverend Morison who was instructed in the way to happiness.

Within the three inclosures were the houses of the village settlement. No doubt they were the buildings which, repaired and maintained with care, had been there for centuries. Each of the five tenants had his dwelling, a barn, a byre, a store for his "best effects", and "a porch on each side of the door to keep off the rain or snow". The walls were of stone, and the roof was thatched with straw and held down by ropes weighted with stones. These low, compact clusters of huts huddled on the open southwest slope of Rona, much like stunted island plants, drab and bedraggled in the dark winter storms, cheerful and open in the long summer daylight.

The restricted size of the population of the island meant that no further "inclosure" had to be added and that no extra demand was made of the land, but it produced complications where marriage and children were concerned. However, in-breeding among the "ancient race" was not inevitable as the Reverend Morison found. At the time of his visit "two of the natives courted a maid with intentions to marry her". She picked one of them while the minister was there, no doubt so that he could marry them, and the other one, unsuccessful, was more than disappointed for "there was no other match for him in this island". Another man who wanted a wife had "got a shilling from a seaman that happened to land there" and gave this shilling to the minister "to purchase him a wife in the Lewis, and send her to him, for he was told that this piece of money was a thing of extraordinary value". Mr Morison set off back to Ness with a fair wind, taking the shilling with him, but after three hours the wind changed and the boat had to return to Rona. When he landed the unsuccessful suitor was delighted to see him back for he had come up with an idea which required the minister's approval: "I bless God and Ronan that you are returned again, for I hope you will now make me happy, and give me a right to enjoy the woman every other year by turns, so that we both may have issue by her". Perhaps this had happened before on Rona, but if so it must have helped to confuse relationships, and Mr Morison, though he "could not refrain from smiling at this unexpected request", rebuked the poor man for what he considered an "unreasonable demand" and asked him to be patient for a year, for on the next summer's boat he could send him also a Lewis wife. This did not satisfy the man "who was tormented with the thoughts of dying without issue". In the end, however, the only recorded outcome was a Lewis wife for the man with the shilling.

How fortunate Mr Morison was, in visiting Rona when it was still inhabited by such people. Within a year or two disaster overtook them, and they were gone. Martin Martin, writing down about 1700 what Morison and "several natives of Lewis who had been upon the place" could tell him, said that about fourteen years before "a swarm of rats . . . came into Rona, and in a short time ate up all the corn in the island". No one knew how they got there. A few months later, some seamen landed and robbed the people of their one bull. Thus deprived of their own resources, and without any chance of a supply from Lewis for a year, the people starved. "These misfortunes", said Martin, "occasioned the death of all that ancient race . . ."[56]

The Steward of St. Kilda's story

So passed away the old days of Rona. Yet something is left. The crumbling remains of the three inclosures still lie on the slope below the graveyard, the chapel and the cell. Angus Gunn's tales still open a narrow window upon the green island home of the holy man, and the account of Monro, all too brief as it is, survives as a small clue to a great mystery. Those who lived in Ness at the time of the starvation must have discovered soon enough what had happened and were able to hand on the story to succeeding generations.

Some time after the dreadful events, it chanced that the island of Lewis heard a remarkable report of the situation in Rona, from a most unexpected source. Martin's brief mention of it conceals more than it tells:

> "The steward of St Kilda being by a storm driven in there [i.e. Rona], told me that he found a woman with her child on her breast, both lying dead at the side of a rock".[57]

There is much to wonder at in these words. What was it like being driven by a storm more than a hundred miles off course? What were the chances of the steward fetching up safely in such a tiny spot as Rona? What was it like there? How did he get home again? Only Mr John MacLeod, tacksman and steward of St. Kilda, could answer such questions, and it is fortunate that he survived to tell the tale of his adventures.[58]

> "On one particular time . . . Mr MacLeod sailed with his Boat from Harris for St. Kilda. He brought his wife in the Boat with him at this time and also a good crew; they landed safe upon the Island and settled with the Tenants. He set sail for home but ere they got half channels, the wind turned in a contrary course and blew high".

The story begins, and men like Martin who crossed the ocean between Harris and St. Kilda could well picture the surging, whitened sea that raged round Mr MacLeod's open boat. The only thing to do was "to steer right before the wind", and after running northwards for many hours they found themselves off an island which proved to be "Rona-a-taiff", Rona of the Ocean. Somehow they all got ashore, and managed to salvage the grain, cheese, tallow, and other stores they had in the boat, but "though they used every mean in their power yet they could not save the Boat for she broke to pieces upon the first day they landed in this Island".

Going up the slopes they came to the remnants of Rona's ancient people:

> "they found a Kind of a House, by which they could perceive this house to have been lately occupied by human beings, and by making farther search through this House they found a woman dead, and a child dead close to her Breast, with his mouth set on his dead Mother's Breast — a melancholly scene indeed; and by farther progress on this island the Husband of this woman, they found dead also. Mr Macleod buried those corpse — after they struck fire, they went round the Island and by this survey they discovered no place that they could save their lives in by a Boat but in the very place in which providence directed them to land and they likewise discovered that a plague of Rats had consumed the Crop upon this Island and in consequence of this failure in the crop, they said that those deceased persons aforesaid died of want. The broken pieces of the Boat was the next thing to be preserved: and as they had plenty of grain which they brought from St. Kilda (and luckily they found a hand mill or Quern) they thus made meal, and did not want as to sustinence".

For seven months the MacLeods and their crew lived upon "this Barren or desolate island". During their "captivity" there, imprisoned by the sea and the wind and the loneliness, they carefully gathered together all the pieces of wood which the sea cast up, and kept a fire going, like the Rona people of old, of whom it was said "They have no fewel for fire upon the Island; but by the special providence of God the sea yearly casts in so much timber as serves them".[59] The MacLeods had another use for driftwood also, for, "as providence ordered it", one of the crew was a carpenter, who, "though he was short of Tools, and had only one handsaw, an Axe, and a gimlet", was able to fashion a boat of the timber washed up and out of the rescued pieces of the old boat. To preserve the wood and seal the cracks he made a tar out of the tallow mixed with ashes. In this way the marooned company found a means of returning home.

When April came, and the winter darkness had given way to some brighter, calmer weather, the MacLeods and their crew set off south, and came into Stornoway without mishap. Everyone had long given them up for lost, but soon the news of their return reached Harris, and great was the stir that it caused. Friends and relatives gathered in Stornoway, and the feast and celebration lasted "for some days". Among the guests was the Lewis factor, Mr Zachary MacAulay, who, on hearing Mr MacLeod's account of his experiences, asked him if he would sell the boat which brought him from Rona. "No", said MacLeod, "I'll preserve the Boat while I live, for I think I would not be considered a man worthy of a miraculous escape from the perils of the Sea were I to sell that Boat for any money whatever".

Mr MacAulay wanted to hear the story again.

"Come, Mr MacLeod, tell us something about your late voyage".

> "Well, . . . upon that day we sailed from Pabbay in Harris, for St. Kilda, we ran the distance in the short time of eight hours . . . as we sailed through a great bank of herrings, a gannet which was diving for those herrings, was pointing for to dive. Just as our boat was sailing fast through this Bank of herrings, he came with such force and right through a plank in the boat, he forced his head; and this gannet though he killed itself thus, yet he stuck into the hole and we allowed him remain till we landed at St. Kilda".

"It is said", MacLeod went on, "that never a Boat or Boat's Crew was drowned going or coming back from that Island, But . . . I would rather be in Rona . . ."

The steward explained that he liked Rona — in spite of the unintended seven months he spent there — because it was so fertile, "so very prolifick", that most ewes, cows and mares gave birth to two offspring at a time, "and so very productive is that Island that I think my wife will soon produce twins".

The listening company laughed heartily at this, and Mr MacAulay expressed the hope that if Mrs MacLeod were delivered of a boy she would call him Ronan.

"Did you do anything whilst you was in that Island", asked

MacAulay, "to keep in remembrance the mercies which you and yours have received . . .?" "I did nothing", came the answer, "to keep my captivity in mind to those who may land there successively after this — only I left a lump of stone on the top of another stone and with this designation, say 'McLeods Lift'. And . . . in order to show that I do not or did not forget that merciful deliverance . . . were that child of mine, who is as yet in his mother's womb, to be a boy, and that he and I would be permitted to live till such a time, I would do my best to make a clergyman out of him, and moreover I would put him in mind of the late dangerous voyage, his own conception likewise as having happened in the Island of Rona, when his parents were in captivity . . ."

"Well" said Mr MacAulay, "I commend you for such a resolution; since that incident which brought about that child's conception in a remote Island . . . will be apt to raise emotions in the mind . . . "

MacAulay agreed that to make the unborn child a clergyman was an excellent idea, and that the strange circumstances of his conception would convince him of the Divine Mercy. After "these festive days" were over Mr MacLeod and his family sailed away to Harris, and in the course of time a boy was indeed born, and, inevitably, made a clergyman. It was said that "he had the Parish of the Rosses in the Island of Mull", and that he was a good minister who "frequently spoke of Rona a taiff as the place of his conception" and regularly used the remarkable story his parents had told him as an illustration in his sermons. It was also said "that that stone aforesaid, McLeod's Lift at Rona, no man was able to lift this stone since McLeod left it at Rona. It is called Fhear-Irt's Lift — or his 'Ultach'". The "St. Kilda Tacksman's Lift" is not known today, and perhaps the weather has toppled the upper stone, but, fortunately, Mr MacLeod's wish to commemorate his adventure through his son and his stone can still be fulfilled through the re-telling of the tale.

PART II

TENANTS AND CROFTING

New Inhabitants

For a while after all the people were gone, the fertile acres of Rona saw no corn or cattle, and the landlord received no further contribution packed into the sheepskin bags. The island's history breaks off as if one of those many banks of ocean mist had drifted across everything. In such circumstances it is even possible to doubt the exactness of what Martin Martin and the St. Kilda tacksman said about the end of the "ancient race", and no one else came along to report on events that may have followed. It appears that an attempt was soon made to repopulate the island, an attempt that ended in a further disaster. Martin reported that some years after the deaths by starvation, the minister, who seems to have held the island from the Earl of Seaforth, "sent a new colony to this island, with suitable supplies". But only a year later a boat dispatched by him with more supplies and "orders to receive the rents" was lost; so Martin had heard, and he could give "no further account of this late plantation".[60] What really happened may be recorded in a tale told about 1850 by Donald MacLeod, probably known as Dòmhnull Ruadh, who had lived on Rona for a year.

> "it is a well sustained and correct tradition that six men with their wives and families, resided here about 200 years ago, and that the men when on a Seal excursion were drowned in Poll Halher [i.e. Heallair], on the southern shore of Rona. Their families after remaining on the Island for six Months after the catastrophe were brought to the Lewis, by the Boats which then annually visited the Island".[61]

This tradition had been heard by Dr John MacCulloch some forty years earlier, since he explained the disappearance of the old population by noting that "In attempting to land on a stormy day, all the men were lost by the upsetting of their boat".[62] MacCulloch's informant, Kenneth MacCagie, also told him about this boat, which they "contrived to house in some cranny on the southern point".[63] If the old story of starvation was indeed true, then it would seem that five or six families had been sent by the minister to live on Rona after the St. Kilda tacksman's adventures there. Given time they might have arranged their affairs in much the same way as those who had died out before. But the second disaster happened, so that again Rona was deserted. And what then? According to Donald MacLeod the island was not abandoned for long.

> "The next person who inhabited it is said to have been a female in whose favour a miracle had been wrought under the following circumstances. It being an old and well received tradition in the Lewis that 'Fire never quenched on Rona' this dame resolved to test its truth but to her consternation found it to be a fallacy — however after offering up some fervant

prayers her fire was relighted by supernatural agency. After this occurrence it was inhabited from time to time by individuals to whom nothing remarkable occurred though some of them resided on it for 5 and some 7 years".[64]

By "individuals" was clearly meant single families as well as the occasional solitary man or woman. In 1764 there were nine people reckoned to be living on Rona, probably all members or servants of one family,[65] much like the arrangement about 1790 when there was a family whose task it was to send to Lewis each year an unspecified quantity of wild fowls, feathers, corn, butter and cheese, a few sheep and sometimes a cow.[66] This contribution, consisting of the same kinds of produce as had formed the Rona rent two hundred years earlier, must have been of sufficient value to make it worth maintaining people in such a remote place, and faith in the island's fertility has persisted ever since.

The idea that someone could be conveniently "lost" from Lewis by sending him or her to Rona is at least as old as the affair of Cornelius Con, and may be said to go back to St. Ronan himself. It was possible for an "exile" to lodge with the family on the island, or to make do on his own. According to Donald MacLeod, in 1850 there still lived in Ness a woman who had been "transported" to Rona from Lewis about 1810 — "whether for theft or general bad conduct, is not generally known";[67] while J.W. Dougal, who went out to Rona for a day in 1927, heard of an even more severe fate, when for some offence a woman was expelled from Rona to the inaccessible Sula Sgeir, whither she was taken by Rona men in their boat and where eventually her skeleton was found with a bird's nest in the cavity of the chest*.[68] Donald MacLeod also said that at some unknown time "a man was transported from Rona to Sulisker for stealing sheep and that he died on the latter place for want of sustenance".[69] About 1850 the island was offered to the Government as a penal settlement, and in 1884-5 it was the temporary home of two men who had excluded themselves from the community of Ness. There were evidently two characteristics of Rona that appealed when the subject of exile came up; it was suitably far away, and it was certainly habitable.

For much of the eighteenth century, however, Rona was quietly occupied by a single family, who went out there voluntarily or after persuasion, and who lived in one of the three ancient "inclosures" on the slope below the graveyard and the chapels. The old system of tenancy had gone with the drowning at Poll Heallair, and a new arrangement was established whereby the island, having been considered as belonging to Habost, came to be part of Swainbost farm in

* This is a reference to Brianuil, St. Ronan's sister.

The north part of the Isle of Lewis showing the Ness distr
and location of places mentioned in the text.

1 The Butt of Lewis (Rudh' Eoropaidh)
2 Cunndal
3 (Port) Stoth
4 Teampull Ronain (Ronaidh)
5 Teampull Mholuaidh
6 Eoropie
7 Fivepenny
8 Knockaird
9 Geodha Chruidh
10 Port of Ness
11 Lionel
12 Habost
13 Swainbost
14 Teampull Pheadair
15 Skigersta (Skegirsta)
16 Cross
17 Baile Glom
18 North Dell and Baile Griais
19 South Dell
20 Dell Mill
21 Eorodale
22 Adabroc
23 Cuiashader
24 Ben Dell
25 Beinn na Caorach
26 Cuile Totair
27 Barvas
28 North Tolsta
29 Muirneag

(Scale of sketch: 1/4 inch / 1 mile.)

Numbers circled are villages
  † : chapels (teampull)
  △ : hills

N

NESS

Numbers 1, 2, 3, 9 : coastal features (headland, bays)
other numbers : one or two buildings only.

Ness, the tenant of which employed a man and his family to look after the stock there and to ensure that the usual variety of produce was stacked ready to load when the boat arrived. The tenant had to pay a rent for Rona, a small sum which in the 1790s was but £4 a year; while the family living on the island was not expected to contribute rent but instead received a proportion of the butter, grain, wild fowls and other "crops" as a wage.[70] Life on Rona must be imagined, for it is not described by anyone until early in the nineteenth century; but it is not difficult to picture an existence which, though much lonelier than it had been in the days when five families kept each other company in all weather, could not be so very different from that of the "ancient race". Birds were hunted on the cliffs, crops were harvested from the "fields", sheep were looked after, all according to long established custom and practice within the limits imposed by seasons and the nature of the island. Perhaps the most noticeable difference was that a community was no longer there, so that the divisions of the shore and the services at the chapel belonged to the past, and the Rona family had the whole island to itself.

The Murrays, Tenants of Rona

The surname of Murray is one of the commonest in Ness.[71] One Murray family was distinguished locally over many generations by the additional name of "Gobha", smith. This description was given because it was understood that the first of the line had been a blacksmith, and some later generations were also smiths. The original smith was called in tradition "An Gobha Gorm", the "blue" smith, and it has been suggested that he was the Murray who crossed the Minch and introduced the clan to the island of Lewis. Traditionally An Gobha Gorm is looked upon as the first of the family to settle in Ness, but not much is known about him.

There are stories still known in Ness explaining why he was called "An Gobha Gorm". One reason put forward was that he had a blue birthmark down the side of his face and neck. Another was given by a person living in Eoropie some years ago, who said that, when a boy, An Gobha Gorm was apprenticed in Ireland. There were many others learning the skills of the blacksmith from the same master. A man came to the smithy to have a sword mended. When he returned to collect it the following day, he tested it by striking it on the anvil, and it broke. He gave it to one apprentice after another, and each time the testing blow broke the sword. Finally the sword was given to the youngest apprentice, the future "Gobha Gorm", whose repair survived the test. The smith promoted the lad by giving him first place at the door after making the others move along. This resulted in his becoming the object of jealousy, and when he went next morning into the smithy, and blew the bellows, the fire exploded in his face, leaving it puckered and blue. Feeling that his life was in danger, the boy fled from Ireland and came to Ness, where he established a smithy of his own at Swainbost.[72]

A similar tale to this relates how the man called "An Gobha Gorm" was a smith in Wick. At a fair held there on one occasion each local smith was given a piece of metal from which he had to make a needle, and the best needle would win its maker a prize. That made by An Gobha Gorm was the most skilfully fashioned in its point and eye and won the competition. The following day the prizewinner went to light his fire in the forge. A jealous rival had put shot in the fire, and as the flames rose the shot exploded, marking the smith's face so that it was blue and ugly. As a result An Gobha Gorm fought a duel with his enemy and killed him. Fearing for his own life he fled to Lewis with a man called MacKay, and they came to Knockaird, where Morrison, known as the Brieve, upholder of the law in Ness, allowed them to stay and, as the custom was, asked no questions of them for a year. During this time An Gobha Gorm took up his former occupation, building a smithy at Cnoc na Ceàrdaich on the Swainbost machair. The site is not far from the present farmhouse and lumps of iron slag can still be found there.[73]

There is still doubt about the full name of An Gobha Gorm, but it is likely that he was William Murray, who, in July 1608, was involved in a fight in Dornoch churchyard. He was wounded in the face by Charles Pape, one of three unpopular brothers, and in return he killed Charles. The other two Papes were severely injured by a John MacPhail and his uncle. William Murray fled from Dornoch and was still alive and free in 1630. In one Ness tradition An Gobha Gorm came from Dornoch, and according to another his arrival with "Iain Mòr MacAoidh" did not happen unnoticed. One day watchers on the coast saw a strange boat rounding the Butt of Lewis and making for the bay of Cunndal, sheltered from easterly winds. Two men came ashore and were immediately taken to the chief of the Morrisons at "the big house of Habost", where they told their tale and were then given asylum. One of the men was An Gobha Gorm, the other was Iain Ruadh MacPhàil, or John MacPhail, one of those involved in the fight with the Pape brothers. One explanation of the fact that the second man was also called MacKay is that the MacPhails of Sutherland were considered a sept of the MacKays.

Whatever the true history of Murray's coming to Ness, it seems certain that he was known by the appearance of an injured face, and that he set up a smithy at Swainbost. He is supposed to have visited

Sula Sgeir and to have been to Rona where he put an iron mooring ring in a rock. About the middle of the 17th century he died and was buried, according to Angus Gunn, "under that big stone which lies between St. Peter's Church in the Swainbost burying ground and the river". Two nameless generations are reckoned to have followed An Gobha Gorm and to have carried on the blacksmith's trade, before the appearance of Neil Murray, called "Niall Gobha" and "Neil Gow" in a rental of 1726. Neil was recorded as tenant in Swainbost in 1718 and 1726.

So early in the 18th century this family of Murray was associated with Swainbost as tenants in the farm there, and it was to this farm that Rona was joined. In 1726 Neil's son, William, known as "Uilleam Mac Neill Ghobha", was also a tenant in Swainbost, and in 1740 he obtained a tack of both Swainbost and Rona, paying a new rent of £4 for the latter.[74] He had married Elizabeth MacKenzie and they had at least two sons, one of whom, Roderick or "Ruaidhri Gobha", succeeded as tacksman and blacksmith not long after his father's early death in 1752. William's widow, called "Widow Muray" and "William Murray Relict" in the records, held the tack in 1755 and shared it with her son Roderick ("Rory") until at least 1771.[75]

As regards Ness farms at this time it appears that the landlord found it more convenient to deal with a single tacksman than with possibly several tenants, each holding a small proportion of the land. William Murray, as tacksman of Swainbost, received rents from the tenants and paid a sum himself to his landlord as a condition of the tack. This arrangement was taken on by Roderick, and evidence given in August 1754 shows how it worked. One of the tenants, "Hugh Bayne", was asked "what Rent the Tack of Swanibost pays yearly to the Tacksman". He answered "That the Town of Swanibost Consists of Six penies lands, that four penies thereof is possesst by ten Tenents and the other two possesst by the Tacksman, That each half penie pays Twenty pound Scots Money Rent yearly so that the Six penies amounts to two houndred and fourty pound Scots yearly money Rent". In earlier years ten days service, twenty hens and ten pecks of meal had also been part of the rent of each tenant, but these were now converted to a sum of 13s 4d scots (1 merk), and each "half penie" paid 3 merks (£2 scots) in mill dues. Hugh, who had lived at Swainbost for fourteen years, added that "the Isleand of Rona is in the Tacksman's possession and that they pay no Services to their Master" for it. The tenants, he said, refused to pay "Entrie" money either, as the island had been part of Swainbost for several years. Another tenant who had been at Swainbost for the same length of time, "Murdo Mcfinlay Roy", confirmed all that Hugh had stated. From similar evidence on the position at Habost it would seem that the addition of Rona to

c1930. Home of the Murrays, tenants of Rona — Swainbost farmhouse, before later alterations.
(photo. Swainbost Farm Collection)

Swainbost had occurred not too many years previously and that the composition of "the Town of Habost", which "consisted of Seven penies land before Rona and Skerstey (Skigersta) was taken of(f) it", remained the same.[76]

Roderick, who seems to have been an educated man, married Jane, daughter of Alexander Morrison, tacksman of Shader in Point. He was tacksman at Swainbost for many years, until at least 1792, and was apparently a successful farmer. In 1767 he built a new house later altered and improved to form the present building, and moved from his former dwelling which he left standing undemolished. The site of the old house was in a field near the new one, and about 1900 there were still some who could remember the old thatched place with gables and whitewashed walls.

An anvil used by Roderick is believed still to exist in Ness, and he was evidently one of the many local whisky distillers, as in 1780 an inventory includes a still and "one old worm" on loan from "Rory Murray in Ness". From 1787 the farm was shared with his brother John, for in that year the tack was made out to Roderick and John Murray, "Wherof the former ⅔rds and the latter ⅓rd, with the whole island of Rhona to Rodk".[77] In January 1792 Rory Murray's household numbered fourteen people and John Murray's seven.[78]

41

The chapel and old graveyard of Teampull Pheadair, Swainbost, former Ness burial ground. Between the chapel and the wall above the stream is the burial place of Alasdair Mac Ruairidh and other Murrays of the Gobh Family.

(photo. Author's Collection)

Roderick Murray had at least three sons, two of whom, Alexander and Donald, were concerned with Rona. The eldest was Alexander, generally known as "Alasdair mac Ruairidh Ghobha". He was the last one of the family to be tacksman of Swainbost and smith there. Depending on which tradition is accepted, he was the seventh or eighth Murray in direct succession from An Gobha Gorm. On 15th December 1814 he married Margaret, one of the twenty children of Kenneth MacIver, tacksman of North Tolsta, whose numerous family was said to have only once sat down at table all together. Educated like his father in Gaelic and English, and as influential in Ness, Alexander died on 16th November 1857, aged 86, and was buried beside his ancestors on the south side of Teampull Pheadair at Swainbost, where a table stone marks the grave.

Alexander gave up Swainbost farm about 1830 and removed to the farm of Dell, otherwise called North Dell, which had been tenanted by a man called Donald Morrison, Dòmhnull Mac Ailean. Here was born in 1834 his son Donald, more commonly known as Daniel or Danny, the only one to remain at home for any time. In an age of emigration Daniel's brothers Kenneth and Colin went out to India as tea-planters, as did Daniel himself eventually, and another brother, Alexander, went to America.* At his death the father Alexander was rentalled for North Dell farm and for Rona, and Daniel succeeded to the tenancy at a rent of £30 per annum and to his father's unpaid rent arrears.[79]

Daniel Murray kept two boats for visits to the islands, by one of which T.S. Muir was landed on Rona from the yacht "Hawk" in July 1860, when Murray was paying a short visit for clipping the sheep. Muir observed that Sula Sgeir was also "farmed" by Murray, and it is evident that this rock, like Rona, had been long in the possession of the family. In 1862, after only four or five years, Daniel Murray gave up the farm at Dell and departed for India where he became a tea-planter in Darjeeling. He did not lose the two islands, since just before he left he entered upon a new seven year lease of Rona and Sula Sgeir, sharing them with his mother, Margaret, and arranging that his sister's husband, John Nicholson, who lived in Stornoway, should pay the rent of £20.[80] The farm of Dell was divided into crofts, and a lot of 23 acres towards the sea called Baile Glom, which was taken by William Watson for £24 rent. After a few years Daniel paid a brief visit home, and, along with his mother, was granted a new lease of the islands for the same length of time and the same rent, to begin in 1872.[81] Margaret Murray died in 1878, while Daniel and his wife, having returned to India, died of cholera only four years later.

Daniel Murray's relatives were not happy at the thought of losing Rona, now separated from its traditional role as part of a Ness farm, but it was Finlay MacKenzie, a tailor with a general merchant's shop in Habost, who with Norman MacKenzie, farmer and fisherman also of Habost, rented Rona for three years from 1884 until 1887. During this period two Ness men died in unusual circumstances on the island, and Finlay MacKenzie gave notice on 6th December 1886 that he and Norman were going to give up the lease.[82] It is said that Daniel's brother Colin then persuaded his cousin, Farquhar Murray, to take over, and in 1887 Farquhar paid his first annual rent in advance, a sum of £12.10s.

Farquhar Murray's father, Donald, was second son to Roderick and younger brother of Alexander, Alasdair Mac Ruairidh. He was born about 1790 and became a cooper in Stornoway, but left this trade and for nineteen years worked on patrol boats pursuing contraband cargoes. He would have received a pension after his twentieth year, but, with only weeks to go, a block fell on his foot, crippling him, and

---

* The family of the mother, the MacIvers of North Tolsta, also went to India as tea-planters.

he was fired at once. He married, as his second wife, Catherine, daughter of Farquhar Smith, tacksman of Earshader, Uig, a man who had six daughters and one son. About 1832 Donald and his family settled on a croft in North Dell. There were at least three daughters and one son, the latter being Farquhar, who was born in 1828. The eldest daughter, Jane, born in 1826, married in 1850 John Gunn, whose croft was the old number 8 North Dell.

By 1856, and possibly as early as 1840, Donald Murray was dead and the croft was held by his widow.[83] Farquhar Murray was a wheelwright and joiner and carried on this trade from the family croft, which is said to have been between numbers 20 and 21 North Dell, although from 1856 to 1867 his widowed mother was rentalled for the old number 20. About 1880 he is supposed to have acquired number 5, and he was rentalled for this croft in 1887, when it was noted that it had been composed out of the old numbers 9 and 22. Farquhar was at that time a township "constable", for which he was allowed 5s off his rent. His sister, Jane Gunn, now a widow and mother of Donald and John Gunn, known as "balaich 'An Guinne", lived at what from 1868 was number 19, but died in 1889 when she was succeeded in the croft by her elder son Donald, who resided in Stornoway during the 1890s.[84]

About 1890 Farquhar Murray entered into a partnership arrangement with Donald and John Gunn, and Donald Weir of 39 Swainbost who had married Farquhar's sister Dolina. They were to share the tenancy of Rona and Sula Sgeir but it is clear from a letter he wrote in January 1892 that Farquhar did not always find it easy to manage the two remote islands. In this letter he acknowledged receipt of requests from the factor for payment of overdue rent, and explained to him that his "sole reason for leaving a balance on the last occasion of payment is that other people, as you are probably aware, are taking possession of these Islands, and that at the very Season of the year, when they are and ought to be of the greatest benefit to me. This State of things is and has been going on for the last three years at least, and that with the full Knowledge of your immediate predecessor in office, but I full[y] expected on your appointment, that my interests as well as Lady Mathesons in these islands would be duly and fully protected — yet these people to whom I have already referred have acted this year just as they have done for the previous two years". He named the offenders, and may have won some satisfaction; but it may also be that the assistance of "balaich 'An Guinne" and Donald Weir provided a way out of the dispute.[85]

Farquhar Murray married Catherine, daughter of Angus Campbell in number 4 North Dell and composer of the song "Cùl do Chinn". They had a family of four sons and two daughters, the eldest son being

Donald, who took over the share of Rona after his father's death in February 1911. Catherine died early in 1877 from typhus fever.

Donald Murray, married to Kate MacDonald of 20 North Dell, was also a joiner and wheelwright, as were his cousins Donald and John Gunn, "balaich 'An Guinne". The same tenant partnership continued, until it was gradually broken by the deaths of the partners. Donald Murray died in 1926, aged 59, leaving a son Murdo, who was only 14. A short while before his death Donald went to see Alex MacFarquhar, tenant of Dell Mill, and asked him if he would take over the controlling interest in Rona, seeing that Murdo was so young, and as a result MacFarquhar bought all three shares of the stock. Later one share was given to Murdo because of his family's close links with the island.

Alex MacFarquhar was the third generation of his family to occupy Dell Mill. His grandfather, Robert, the first MacFarquhar in Lewis, came from Redcastle in the Black Isle to Stornoway as a building contractor. His son, Alexander, became tenant of Dell Mill about 1853, and was rentalled for it until 1867 at a rent that rose from £45 to £58 in 1860, possibly because more ground was taken into the mill lands.[86] In 1868 Alexander committed suicide, and the lease of the mill was taken over by his brother Murdo, who developed the mill lands as a farm by enlarging and repairing the house now called "Dell Farm House", buying the stock of emigrating Dell crofters, and building a march dyke between his farm and the North Dell crofts. He was succeeded by his son Alexander — "Alex" — who took over Rona about 1926. Alex became a well known, rather eccentric figure in Ness, and was pictured by Robert Atkinson as he was one wet morning on Rona in 1936, "a tall man with rain dripping from his somewhat straggly moustache".[87]

The partnership between Alex MacFarquhar and Murdo Murray continued until 1939, when Murdo entered the Navy at the beginning of the Second World War. At this point Donald MacLeod from Eoropie, who had married Murdo's sister, took over the Murray share and worked the island along with Alex MacFarquhar. In August 1941 Murdo came home on what was to prove his last leave. He went out to Rona with the others in a Polish naval vessel, in order to clip sheep and take off some as no-one had been there for two years. A month later he was killed, and the ancient association of the Murray family with Rona was broken for ever.

With Murdo's death, Donald MacLeod's participation became all the more important to Alex MacFarquhar who was getting elderly and less able to do the strenuous work involved in the tenancy of Rona. After the end of the war, they were joined by a man already familiar with the sheep on the island, John MacKenzie from Swainbost farm,

Alex MacFarquhar contemplating at the sheep pen, Leathad Fhianuis. Beside him is a sack of the clipped wool.
(photo. Comunn Eachdraidh Nis Collection)

The Ness shepherds having their mid-day meal on North Rona in July 1927. Sitting second from right is Murdo Murray (Murchadh Dhomhnuill Fhearchair), the last of the Murrays to be a tenant of Rona.

(photo. see J.W. Dougall opp. p.161)

47

who took one of MacFarquhar's two shares. Well before MacFarquhar died, however, it was felt that the whole business of keeping sheep on Rona, with the necessary hire of a boat as well as considerable inconvenience, was uneconomical and awkward to manage, so the stock was sold to the Ness crew of a fishing boat, the "Queen of the Isles", skipper Donald Gunn, and in this way the farming of Rona became associated, as it still is, with fishermen, a more sensible arrangement which maintains the old link with Ness.

The Murrays' Boat

The association of the family of An Gobha Gorm with Rona and Sula Sgeir was a long one, beginning before the lease of Rona granted to William Murray in 1740. The old system under which a group of small tenants lived on Rona had died with the starvation and drowning of the people, and was replaced with the tenancy of the Murrays who, because the landowner was a remote and little known figure, sometimes almost seemed to be the actual owners of the island. T.S. Muir wrote of his "valuable friend . . . Mr Daniel Murray, in whose family Rona, as parcel of the Butt farm of North Dell, has been for generations",[88] and in his letter Farquhar Murray, giving a "brief resume of the somewhat ancient history of the islands of Rona and Sulisker", stated that his ancestors "with the exception of a very short interval, have possessed them for the last two hundred years or more and had always the Island of Sulisker especially for the wild fowls".[89] It is quite likely that the connection between the Murrays and Sula Sgeir went back to the days of An Gobha Gorm himself, and when Murdo Murray died in 1941 it was a very old link that was broken.

When the Murrays were at Swainbost they paid their rent to the factor representing MacKenzie of Seaforth. To collect the produce of Rona they maintained a large open boat, which was remembered in the late nineteenth century by Murdo MacDonald.

"Rona from time immemorial belonged to the Lewis Estate. It was held by a family of the name of Murray on rent or as part of the farm of Swainbost, Ness, for more than 100 years. There would sometimes be 18 head [of] cattle and 100 sheep on Rona. Cheese made on Rona was considered superior to what was made at home [i.e. in Ness] but Butter Harsh and Oily tasted in my early days they used to go to Rona 3 or 4 times in the summer season with a large Boat having 16 oars for the produce of the island such as cattle, sheep, wool, Butter, cheese, Feathers, oil".

Alexander Carmichael heard that this boat was manned by a crew of twentyone men, and that it was "a long open galley of some eight or ten burthens". The crew consisted of "skilled neighbours from Ness" who, in addition to offering their services as oarsmen and as herds who

48

would gather sheep, paid 5/– to 7/– for the privilege of killing seals, catching birds and collecting eggs during their stay which might last a week or two and sometimes more if the weather turned bad.

"When the men sat down to their oars they chanted their ocean littany . . . and commended themselves to the three-fold God who rules the ocean waves (Steersman and oarsmen chant alternately):

An Stiùireadair	Beannaichte bitheadh ar long
An Sgioba	Beannaicheadh Dia an t-Athair
An Stiùireadair	Beannaichte bitheadh ar long
An Sgioba	Beannaicheadh Dia am Mac
An Stiùireadair	Beannaichte bitheadh ar long
An Sgioba	Beannaicheadh Dia an Spiorad
Uile	Gum beannaicheadh Dia an Trianaid (n) sinne 's ar long
An Stiùireadair	Ciod is eagal duinn us Dia an t-Athair leinn?
An Sgioba	Chan eagal aon nith
An Stiùireadair	Ciod is eagal duinn us Dia am Mac leinn?
An Sgioba	Chan eagal aon nith
An Stiùireadair	Ciod is eagal duinn us Dia an Spiorad leinn?
An Sgioba	Chan eagal aon nith.

An Stiùireadair
A Dhè! Athair Uile-chumhachdaich
Iosa Mhic nan deur 's na caoidh
Le d' comh-chaomhnadh, O! Spioraid Naoimh:
Am t-Aon Dia, beò, fìor, agus buan,
A thug Clann Isreil trid na Muir Ruaidh
Agus Jonah gu tìr à broin miol-mhòr a' chuain;
A thug Pòl agus 's na tha comhla ris 'san long
A gabhadh na mara agus ànradh nan tonn
'S na stoirm ro-mhòr 's na doinnean ro-throm
Seun, agus saor, agus naomhaich sinne;
'S giulain an sìth sinn gu cean ar nuidhe
Le gaoithe caora ciùin gun fhiaradh gun ansadh,
Nach dèan gniomh fuadach dhuinn

An nith s iarramaid ort a Dhia
A reir do throil 's do bhriathra fèin.

The Steersman	Blessed be our ship
The Men	God the father bless her
The Steersman	Blessed be our ship
The Men	God the Son bless her
The Steersman	Blessed be our ship
The Men	God the Spirit bless her
All	May God the Three-in-One bless ourselves and our ship
The Steersman	What fear can befall us, and God the Father with us?
The Men	No! Not one fear
The Steersman	What fear can befall us, and God the Son with us?
The Men	No! Not one fear
The Steersman	What fear can befall us, and God the Spirit with us?
The Men	No! Not one fear.

The Steersman
God, Father All-Powerful
For love of Jesus Christ thy Son
With the co-assistance of Thy Holy Spirit
The only God, living, true and eternal,
Who took the Children of Israel through the Red Sea
And Jonah to land from the belly of the great Whale;
Who saved Paul and all that were with him in the ship
From the raging waves and the commotion of the deep
And from the great storm and tempest wild;
Shield us, and Save us, and sanctify us,
And carry us in peace to our destination,
With mild gentle winds neither swirling nor eddying
That will do no harmful deeds to us
And this we ask of Thee, O God
According to Thy will and word.

With this preliminary safeguard, the crew set out, and Carmichael said that they helped themselves forward by singing "their ocean songs".[90] It was also remembered in tradition that any group of people, from Rona or from Ness, who were travelling between Lewis and the island, customarily visited the old Teampull Ronaidh at Fivepenny before or after their journey to offer up appropriate prayer. The large boat, which must have had many a hazardous voyage in the eighteenth and early nineteenth centuries, was apparently given up at or soon after the time when the Murrays moved from Swainbost to Dell, and was replaced by smaller craft which involved even greater risks. There seems to be no record or tradition of the boats used by the landlord and the Rona people in the days before the Murrays.

The MacKays and MacRitchies

To manage their affairs on the island, the Murrays sent out a shepherd/crofter, and his family, usually for seven years although sometimes for longer. What little is known about the life of these shepherds before 1800 has already been described. It seems they were commonly connected with Swainbost where the Murrays were farmers and certainly some of those who were on Rona in the early nineteenth century were sent from that "town". The man may well have been a tenant or cottar on Swainbost farm.

The names of these earliest families were not recorded at the time, but there are one or two later clues. In notes on the MacFarlanes in Ness there is mention of the earliest known member of that family to live at Cuiashader.[91] This was John, born about 1720 and father of Norman, whose son Angus was born at Skigersta about 1780 and was killed at Waterloo. It is noted that Angus had been married to "M.

50

Stoth near the Butt of Lewis in Ness, point of landing and departure for Rona travellers.

(*photo. Author's Collection*)

51

MacLeod Rona", sister to Kenneth MacLeod of Rona. Another MacFarlane, living more or less in the same period as Angus, was Malcolm of Cuiashader, and later of Skigersta, whose wife was Mary Campbell, called "Màiri Ceannaich". Mary was the daughter of a John Campbell, who was supposed to have been a merchant in Stornoway and was probably the "John Ceannaich" living at Skigersta in 1792. In a census return Mary is said to have been born in Rona. The MacLeods and the Campbells may therefore have been the families sent to the island about 1780, and it is interesting to find that the name for the old folds west of the houses on Rona was given to the Ordnance Survey originally as "Cro Eoin Cheannich".

The MacKays were the first such family of whom there is any real knowledge. The name MacCagie, or a name known in tradition as MacCadie, was apparently the same as MacKay, but it is not clear whether the line can be traced back to the MacKay (MacPhail) who came to Ness with An Gobha Gorm. This MacKay, Iain Ruadh or Iain Mòr, is said to have been a big strong man; he was supposed to have married a girl of Rona, though others say he married someone from Arnol or Bragar, and to have lived in the Uig district until he was killed by the MacAulays in Bernera.[92] There were few if any MacKays living in Ness. It is also said, however, that shortly after 1800 there were six families of MacCagie or MacCadie in Ness, that one of them went to Rona and that on this family's return from the island they all took the name of MacKay, the other five then leaving for Uig.

In 1792 Fionnlagh Ruadh (MacKay) was living in Swainbost. He is thought to have been the son of either Dòmhnull Ruadh or Iain Ruadh.[93] He married Ann MacRitchie of 3 Lionel, and a son Iain was born at Swainbost in 1801. A few years later, perhaps in 1806, Fionnlagh Ruadh with his wife and son went out to Rona, where four further children were born — Donald in 1806, Malcolm (Calum) in 1808, Catherine in 1810, and a second Donald in 1812 who died in infancy. The family came home in 1813, and the four island children were baptised in that year, with an explanation noted in the register that Fionnlagh Ruadh's "having resided at the remote island of Rona was the cause why his children were so long unbaptised". The next son, Norman, was baptised in 1814 at Swainbost but also died in infancy, and another Norman was baptised there in 1816, but after that the family apparently moved to Lionel where two further children, Henny and Donald, were baptised in 1819 and 1822. It may be that in fact they had moved to FivePenny, because it is said that they went from that village to Skigersta when the crofts were made in 1824, and subsequently Malcolm lived at No 7 FivePenny. According to tradition, Iain married Catherine MacIver, Steinish, and became a crofter/fisherman at Sandwick near Stornoway; the elder Donald went to the mainland fishing, married and settled in or near Helmsdale; Norman became a crofter/fisherman at Skigersta where he later lived at numbers 13/14, occupied until recently by his grandson; and the younger Donald became a man of many skills, fisherman, carpenter and boatman, later living at number 17 Skigersta. Of Malcolm more will be said later, but the fate of another son, Angus, deserves to be recorded even though he had no immediate connection with Rona. Angus went into the Navy and then the Merchant Service, where he was in the late 1830s when he was aged about twenty. At this time he and a lad from Glasgow were on a sailing ship commanded by a Captain Johnstone who came from near Dunnet Head in Caithness. The rest of the crew, described as "foreigners", decided that they were going to get rid of Angus and the Glasgow boy, so they seized them while they were asleep and tied them to the winches, where the two victims were wound to death. It is thought that the cook reported the captain, who was sentenced to twentyone years in prison.*

Not much is known about Fionnlagh Ruadh. He was born in 1777 and was on Rona from 1805/6 to 1812/13. He is supposed to have been a quiet, sensible man, not remarkable for strength or stature, but there is a tradition that when he came back from Rona he had a great beard and a comb or ornament of bone fixed in his hair. When he and his family went to Skigersta they first occupied number 9. In the early 1830s Fionnlagh exchanged crofts with Norman Morrison of 13/14 Skigersta. On his death in 1863 this croft passed to his son Norman, who split it between his sons Norman and Allan. Donald, youngest son of Fionnlagh Ruadh, married twice, first to Margaret Murray (nighean Aonghais 'ic Thormoid) of 28/29 South Dell, by whom he had no family, and second to Catherine Buchanan (nighean a' Phunndair) of 12 North Dell, who was mother to eight children. The oldest son, Malcolm, was a carpenter like his father, and the skill was passed on to Malcolm's son John. Donald took over croft number 17 Skigersta about 1850; it had been formed in 1842, and may have been initially occupied by Donald's brother Norman. In his last years Fionnlagh Ruadh lived with Donald at number 17, where the old joiner's shop still stands, now used as a barn. Fionnlagh Ruadh's eldest son, Iain, was T.S. Muir's companion and informant on visits to Rona in 1857 and 1860. Perhaps Muir made a mistake by saying in his account that Rona was "the spot where Iain first drew breath",[94] but he did record at least some of the information he was given by Iain about the island fifty years earlier, and what he wrote therefore

---

* Captain Johnstone's son was master of a merchant ship in the first World War. The ship was torpedoed and the crew captured, and the captain was put on oath by the German submarine skipper that he would never lift a hand against the Germans. This too was reported and the second Captain Johnstone lost his ticket.

provides a picture — a very limited one — of how the family lived while in its solitude.

Iain told of the ritual associated with candles on the altar and looking at the light through the holes of the stone cross. He remembered it as a little mysterious, for "I was taken away out of Rona before I could know or think very much more about it."[95] He spoke too about hanging wool on the wooden pin within the cell, of the condition of the whole chapel, and of how they kept it in repair. Evidently he had learned the tales of the island for he described to Muir how St. Ronan went there, and he added the story of how the devil went out after him. To him St. Ronan's candles would have been familiar articles — "cuddy-oil candles they were — just what we had in the island; if you were to come in the winter time, you could see them about the Ness, and in the Sandwick houses out-by there — plenty of them". Muir asked Iain for other stories:

"You Eilean Rona folks, Iain, must have had a heap of odd old stories to tell one another, as you gathered round the fire in the long winter nights; for then, I fancy, you had little else to do".

"Nor in the days, neither, often; for sometimes the days and the nights were so alike, you could scarce tell which was which. But in the summer-time it was a bonny place — so green; and you would not see such barley and potatoes as we had, anywhere. There was only a few of us altogether, big and little, and it would be lonely, often: but we were content, and had no strife — if we had, things didn't go right, and if bad words were spoken when we sowed, the seed came never to anything, or it grew black and withered . . ." [96]

This was all Muir's version of Iain's few words, and it is a pity that he did not record more of the daily life on Rona. Iain said he had much more to tell, but Muir did not ask him, or, if he did, put no other details in his books. There are, however, one or two other things that must be said of the family, and perhaps in future more can be added. There is no record of the "transported" woman at this time, but Daniel Murray, living at North Dell about 1860, wrote in a letter that Angus Gunn "was in Rona as assistant to Finlay MacKay, Iain's father",[97] an important piece of information which is related to the handing down of Rona's traditions as well as to Angus Gunn's career, and the reason for his being there with Finlay is itself of interest. Furthermore, some twenty years after the family had returned from Rona, become known as MacKay, and, unlike the other MacCagies, settled in Ness, the third son, Calum, who was born on Rona in 1808, himself became a shepherd on the island and had sons born there.

The MacKays' connection with Rona was not broken with the return of Fionnlagh Ruadh in 1813, for in that same year, and probably with the same boat, there went out a Kenneth MacCagie who was probably Finlay's brother. Kenneth was married to Margaret MacAulay of Swainbost, and it seems they lived in Habost, for a daughter, Catherine, was baptised there in 1812. Two sons were born in Rona, Iain in 1814, and Donald in 1818. The family came back to Swainbost in 1820 and it is believed they took the name of MacRitchie, not MacKay. The daughter Catherine married Calum Murray of Swainbost in 1834 and settled in Cross, but there is little known of the other children. With this family the name MacCagie also seems to be given as MacKiogan or MacGiogan, which became MacKenzie as well as MacRitchie.

It was during the stay of these second MacCagies on Rona between 1813 and 1820 that John MacCulloch made his visit to the island, apparently in 1819. He found that Kenneth MacCagie had been in Rona seven years and that in that time "he had, with the exception of a visit from the boat of the Fortunée, seen no face but that of his employer and his own family".[98] MacCulloch's arrival was therefore a major event in the MacCagies' years, and it was no wonder that they were shy of the meeting.

Dr John MacCulloch, a geologist who spent ten years sailing among the Hebrides, is the first recorded "visitor" to Rona and the first after Martin Martin to provide a description of life there. Setting out from near Cape Wrath one day in autumn, MacCulloch felt as if he were an explorer, for Sula Sgeir and Rona in his time were "scarcely known except to the mariners who navigate the north sea and to the inhabitants of Lewis",[99] and to have visited them "gives a claim to distinction scarcely less in estimation than to have explored the sources of the Nile or the Niger".[100] By the evening the ship was near the islands, but no land could be seen, the weather "proving thick", and so they hove to for the night. In the morning Sula Sgeir was seen about twelve miles to the north and by mid day they had reached Rona lying in the sunshine. There seemed to be only one landing place, probably that on the south coast at Poll Thothatom, made difficult by being at the foot of a cliff washed high with the ocean swell: ". . . it is necessary to be watchful for the moment to jump out on the first ledge of rock to which the boat is lifted by the wave".[101] Having no acquaintance with any easier spot, MacCulloch with some of the crew who were from Argyll and spoke Gaelic landed on the ledge and climbed up the cliff:

"The first objects we saw as we reached the surface of the cliff, were a man and a boy, who, with a dog, were busily employed in collecting and driving away a small flock of sheep. No houses were visible; but, a little further off, we perceived two women, each loaded with a large bundle, who seemed to have arisen out of the ground, and were running with all speed towards the northern side of the island. It was plain that they had taken us for pirates or Americans . . ."[102]

One of the Argyll men called out, and his Gaelic shout "made the shepherd and his boy bring to". There were explanations to set the shepherd's mind at rest, and then some of the visitors made off to explore the island while the sun was still shining and the fine weather lasted. They crossed the ridge and looked down on Fianuis before descending the steep Leathad Fhianuis to Sgeildige where they admired the deep creek and the cave. The coast on the west side of Fianuis showed the marks of the ocean's winter violence, for the land was heavily eroded and the soil washed away "for a considerable space". Elsewhere "The dykes of the sheep folds are often thrown down, and stones of enormous bulk removed from their places, at elevations reaching to 200 feet above the high water mark; so powerful is the breach of the sea". They saw how the rocks at the western extremity ran far out in long flat ledges, and that a similar ledge in the north was partly covered with grass.[103] Then they climbed up the Tòbha and surveyed the whole isle.

MacCulloch felt the loneliness:

> "To sit on this spot, whence no trace of human existence is visible, and to contemplate from such narrow bounds the expanse of water every where meeting the sky, produces a feeling of solitude and abandonment. The ship on the ocean is a world in itself. There, even if alone, we seem to move towards the society we have left, but Rona is for ever fixed in the solitary sea".[104]

The feeling impressed MacCulloch so deeply, as it did others who came after him, that he wrote again:

> "It is the total seclusion of Rona from all the concerns of the world, which confers on it that intense character of solitude with which it seemed to impress us all. No ship approaches in sight; seldom is land seen from it . . . Rona is forgotten, unknown, for ever fixed, immoveable, in the dreary and waste ocean".[105]

Land can be seen quite easily on a good day, when the mountains of Sutherland rise steep and blue on the south-east horizon, but the day when MacCulloch was ashore was one of the many when the ocean mist and the haze of distance limit the view to a few miles of water. At any rate for him Rona was lost in the isolation of the sea, a place which "the map-makers had forgotten . . .".

The visitors then made their way down the Tòbha and along the south facing slope of the island to the point where, "in the middle and elevated part", they could see a few cultivated acres.[106] Kenneth MacCagie and his son, recalled by the Gaelic cries, were chatting to the Argyll men, "but it was some time before the females came from their retreat, very unlike in look to the inhabitants of a civilised world".[107] Then they all assembled on a green knoll, and MacCulloch joined in what he called "the palaver", asking questions of the shepherd by which "I extracted all the political information that related to this territory".[108] This meant that he tried to learn all that MacCagie could tell him about the history and way of life on Rona.

Kenneth MacCagie told how there had been five families on the island until the drowning, "since which time it has been in the possession of a principal tenant in Lewis".[109] Now only the one family was there, and Kenneth went on to explain his own presence and employment. "He is", wrote MacCulloch, "properly speaking, a cottar, as he cultivates the farm on his employer's account".[110] In addition to growing crops on what amounted to six or seven acres, he tended fifty small sheep, and caught birds on the cliffs. This must have been the work of the shepherd families before him, and closely resembled the agricultural system that prevailed in the time of the ancient race. He was bound to his employer for a period of eight years, a condition that seemed to MacCulloch unnecessary in view of the surrounding ocean and the fact that he was not allowed to keep a boat.[111] In return for these services MacCagie was allowed £2 a year, generally paid in the form of clothes for the members of his family, "the use of a cow, which was brought from Lewis when in milk, and exchanged when unserviceable", and a proportion of the crops of barley, oats and potatoes. The family was allowed to consume all the potatoes and as much of the grain crops as it pleased, the surplus, which averaged about eight bolls of barley, going to the tenant along with the wool, ewe milk cheese, and "an annual supply of eight stone of feathers" from the seabirds.[112] The tenant sent out his boat twice a year to take away the barley, the feathers and the produce of the sheep, which were in total the value of Rona to him and which had to amount to more than was needed to cover at least the costs of a £2 wage, a £2 rent, and provision of a boat and crew.[113]

Kenneth MacCagie himself struck MacCulloch as "a good humoured careless fellow, little concerned about tomorrow" and equally unconcerned about the rest of the world.[114] He wished only to have his two younger children christened.[115] The unbaptised children were of course Iain, who at the age of five was helping his father, and Donald, still a baby. MacCulloch found the family to consist of six individuals, the other three being Kenneth's wife Margaret, their daughter Catherine, now aged seven, and "an aged and deaf mother who watched the child and the interior economy".*[116] The remarkable thing about the mother, who must have been Kenneth's, was that she had been on Rona for forty years — "the female patriarch has been forty years on the island" as MacCulloch put it.[117] This suggests that

* In 1819 MacCulloch wrote of the condition of the women, calling "the mother old, and the wife deaf." (Vol.I p.209).

not only was she Fionnlagh Ruadh's mother, but that she and her husband had been on the island for perhaps over twenty years before Fionnlagh Ruadh became a shepherd there, and therefore that both he and Kenneth were born on Rona. The connection of the MacCagies would therefore go well back into the eighteenth century.

"Although our conference had lasted some time", MacCulloch remembered, "none of the party discovered that it was held on the top of the house".[118] It may have been the smoke issuing from a hole in the green knoll that first attracted his attention, and later he felt that the dwelling might "have been constructed for concealment", although he knew that the weather was the real enemy:

> "Such is the violence of the wind in this region that not even the solid mass of a Highland hut can resist it. The house is therefore excavated in the earth, the wall required for the support of the roof scarcely rising two feet above the surface. The roof itself is but little raised above the level, and is covered with a great weight of turf, above which is the thatch; the whole being surrounded with turf stacks to ward off the gales".[119]

Sitting there, MacCulloch may have asked Kenneth MacCagie if the visitors could look inside his house, and perhaps the latter led them to a doorway previously unnoticed:

> "The entrance to this subterranean retreat is through a long, dark, narrow and tortuous passage like the gallery of a mine, commencing with an aperture not three feet high and very difficult to find.* With little trouble it might be effectually concealed; nor, were the fire suppressed, could the existence of a house be suspected, the whole having the appearance of a collection of turf stacks and dunghils".[120]

When the party at last crawled into the main room of the house they found it dark and bare:

> "The interior strongly resembles that of a Kamschatkan hut; receiving no other light than that from the smoke hole, being covered with ashes, festooned with strings of dried fish, filled with smoke, and having scarcely an article of furniture".[121]

The fish hung from wooden rafters holding up the roof of turf and thatch while below them were the ash-covered floor and the fire:

> "There was a sort of platform, or dais, on which the fire was raised, where the old woman and her charge sat; and one or two niches, excavated laterally in the ground, and laid with ashes, seemed to be the only bed places. Why these were not furnished with straw, I know not; and, of blankets, the provision was as scanty as that of the clothes. Possibly, ashes

---

* Elsewhere MacCulloch described the entrance as "an irregular hole, about four feet high, surrounded by turf" (1824 Vol.III. p.319).

The entrance doorway to the passage leading into the main room of the south-west inclosure. It was probably above this that MacCulloch sat talking to Kenneth MacCagie.

(photo. Author's Collection)

may make a better and softer bed than straw; but it is far more likely that Kenneth MacCagie and his family could not be fashed to make themselves more comfortable".[122]

There was no real peat to burn, for if the island had ever had any it had been used up long ago. Peaty turf was cut instead, and smouldered away with only an occasional flame when a dry root caught or a drip of seal oil fell from blubber hanging above. The fire did not add much light to the interior, "cuddies" and seals being used to supply fuel for the "crusie" lamps:

> "The oil of the coal fish served for light and a 'kindling turf' preserved the fire during the night; but had that fire been extinguished . . . no provision was at hand for rekindling it . . . MacCagie only shrugged his shoulders at the suggestion of a flint and steel; he had lived seven years without one".[123]

Without fulmars to hunt on the cliffs there was no bird oil for the crusies, and fulmar feathers did not form a part of the rent payment. Fish and seal oil no doubt served well enough. It is surprising that MacCulloch did not mention seals in his description of the family's domestic life, as these creatures must have been valuable both for their blubber and for their skins, particularly since the annual wage of clothing worth £2 seems to have been less than enough to dress all the six MacCagies. "Covered they are not", wrote MacCulloch. "The younger child and the woman had, for clothing, something in the shape of a blanket, the ancient covering, apparently, of their race, but scarcely sufficient for the most indispensible purposes".[124]

To the visitor, such half naked people seemed primitive indeed, and yet in some ways they were better off than those who were living in Lewis. The island with its good soil was a fertile place, as was well known. For their sustenance, the MacCagies had excellent mutton, and from the ewe milk made cheeses "resembling those for which St. Kilda is so celebrated".[125] They had the cow's milk and cream, good quantities of potatoes, barley and oat meal, fish, and the birds of the island which nested on the cliffs and on easily accessible places like Fianuis and Sceapull:

> "Beside the produce of the farm they are supplied with animal food, in the sea fowl and in the small coal fish [cuddies] which are taken with the rod; and thus, with all their disadvantages, are sure of abundant food, that with which their countrymen in the situation of small tenants are not always provided".[126]

There was a limited but just sufficient supply of water in two or three wells, which MacCulloch did not seem to notice, for he said that "There is no other water in the island than that which is collected in pools from the rain".[127] One well, under the cliff-top edge at Poll

Heallair, ran, and still runs, quite strongly even in dry weather, while another beside a rock on the north-west side of the village could become stagnant like the pools in the turf towards the Tòbha if it was not regularly used.*

Such were the conditions of life on Rona as MacCulloch saw them in 1818 or 1819. The MacCagies were not unhappy at the isolation. "The wife and mother", he thought, "looked as wretched and melancholy as Highland wives and mothers generally do",[128] but the family "appeared to be contented, well fed, and little concerned about what the rest of the world was doing".[129] He wondered "if beings so insulated had no desires to return to society", and found they had none, the children knowing no other life and the father wishing for little that could not be had on Rona save the christening:

> "I shall not be surprised if after the accomplishment of his only wish he should again long for his now habitual home: and expect that some future visitor will twenty years hence find Kenneth MacCagie wearing out his life in the subterranean retreat of his better days".[130]

The afternoon was drawing on, and it being early autumn the weather could not be trusted to hold for long.** The wind and sea were already rising, and MacCulloch, afraid that he might be marooned on the island for the winter, beat a hasty retreat. The visitors had left Kenneth MacCagie all their tobacco, and, since he had free use of the island flock, "he made no scruple, of selling us a sheep".[131] Now in their hurry MacCulloch and his companions thought they might have to leave the sheep behind, but MacCagie knew how to take it down the cliff.

> "The removal of the sheep is a perilous operation, the animal being slung by the legs round the neck of a man and thus carried down the face of a rock where a false step exposes him to the risk of being either strangled or drowned".[132]

Down at the sea's edge MacCulloch nearly missed his jump into the boat, but soon he was safely aboard and the island was immediately in its own separate world. Sailing away for a look at Sula Sgeir, the party gazed back at the rocks and slopes of an island, strangely inhabited, now withdrawing into the wilderness of surging waves and heaving swell — "the stormy and solitary abode of North Rona".***[33]

MacCulloch did not see Rona again. The sheep and the ewe milk cheese were short-lived souvenirs of the place, but he thought that the cheeses alone were worth the voyage. Unfortunately, "having been

---

* It is said that another well once existed on top of the Tòbha.
** MacCulloch noted on his visit that the grain was already "housed" (1824, Vol.III, p.315).
*** This seems to be the first use of the word "North".

taken in the state of curd out of the salt water, and placed straightway in new casks . . . with all the seams well pitched", the cheeses were found on their return to have been "half devoured by mites", and so little pleasure could be derived from them.[134] Perhaps the best reminder of the island was the account which he immediately wrote of his expedition. It was published in 1819, and again in a slightly different form five years later. Whether his account was accurate was a matter for disagreement. Fifty years later Alexander Carmichael thought most of it incorrect, "while much of what is not incorrect is not worth quoting".[135] All that can be said now is that the printed word is not always correct and that MacCulloch should not necessarily be accepted as a better authority than other sources on matters where accounts differ. Neverthless his information is an extremely valuable contemporary record.

The Bard and his family

Kenneth MacCagie and his family left Rona not long after MacCulloch's visit, probably in the spring of 1820. They were succeeded on the island by MacLeods. Angus MacLeod, known as a composer of verses and therefore called "Bard", lived at Swainbost farm and was married to Mary Murray. They had five children born at Swainbost before they went to Rona: Anne (1810), Mary (1812), Cirstina (1815), William (1817), and Donald (1820). Three more children were born on the island, Kenneth in 1822, Iain in 1825, and Catherine in 1826, and it seems likely that they returned to Lewis in 1827 or 1828.

Not much is recorded about the MacLeods, though their descendants are still to be found in Lewis. There is an idea that they were on Rona for a short time, perhaps only a year, but this does not seem to be correct. Rumours went around at the time that Aonghas Bard was killing sheep for his own use without permission, although his predecessors on the island could apparently take one of the flock as they wished, and it must have been difficult for the tenant at Swainbost to know whether a sheep had died during a severe winter, from disease or other natural cause, or at the hands of the shepherd. Angus was naturally annoyed and composed a song of at least twelve verses about the episode:

LATHA FIADHAICH ANN A RONAIDH — le Aonghas Bard
Air Fonn: Chunnaic mi 'n damh donn 's na h-eildean
A' direadh a'bhealaich le cheile

1 Anns a' mhaduinn air Di-ciadaoin
   Chuir mi m' aghaidh rathad Fianuis,
   Dh'fhag mi na h-uain mar bu mhiann leam,
   Rinn mi gnìomh 's cha d'rinn mi glèidheadh.

2 Sud a' mhaduinn a bha meallta,
'S cinnteach mi gun chinnich call leatha,
Bha fear Tholstaidh anns an àm sin
'S e gu teann an ceann a' ghreime.

3 Bha sgiobadh an eathair bhàin ann,
Is mòr a bh'innte de mo chàirdean,
Aonghas Donn 'us Iain Beag Màirtin,
'S fear m' a bràighe — làimh na feuma.

4 Dh'èirich mi moch là Calluinn
'S ann a sud a bha chùis-ghrabha,
Bha muir bàn air feadh a bhaile [Bha am bail' le cop na mara]
Mar an cabhadh anns na speuran.

5 Cha do chaill mi bonn dè m' mhisneachd
Gus na dhìrich e na Sgitean,
Talamh a' Charn is e 'ga bhriseadh,
Mise 's mo phaisdean an èigein.

6 Ach 's diumbach mise de mo chàirdean
Nach do dh'innis iad dhomh mar bhatar
Ged a cheangailt le glas-làmh mi
Cha leiginn bhar fàire an Sgeipear.

7 Chaidh na balaich do'n cheardaich [chairdich]
Dùil aca gur i bu bhlàithe,
Sin an uair thuirt Mac Mhic-Aoidh,
"Mo chreach-sa thàinig! C'àit an tèid mi?"

8 Chaidh mi mach rathad Cro-Fhionnlaigh,
Cha robh clach an sin gun tionndadh,
Cha b'e sin a bha mi 'g ionndrainn,
Cha d'fhuair mi cunntas nan treudan.

9 Bha trì uain ann a bha tlachdmhor,
Bha uan maol na caorach ghlais ann,
Bha fear cùl-ghorm, dubh-ghorm, dait' ann
'S bha fear ac' air dhreach an t-slèibhe

10 An saol sibh fèin nach mòr an nàire
Dh'fhear a leughadh Beurla 's Gàidhlig
Dhol a dh'èigheachd ormsa mearlach
Airson bàthadh Geodha Meura?

11 Is mòr agaibh fein a' Mhineach,
Mar i as fheàrr tha ann ur Sgìre, [Ma's i a's fearr tha ann 'ur sgire]
Thug an oidhch' ud uams' de chaoraich
Na chuireadh prìs air an fhèill dhith [diubh];

12 An uair a ruigeas mi mo dhùthaich,
'Sa theannas tu 'ga mo spuilleadh [gu mo spiulladh]
An uair a ruigeas tu mo luireach [ruisgeas]
★Bheir mi crùn dhuit chionn a leughadh.

★ Song taken down by Angus L. MacDonald from Angus Gunn, Lionel, 12 August 1927. A version is also preserved in the "Bard" family.

Notes:

Fianuis — the north end of the island below "Leathad Fianuis".

Fear Tholstaidh — one of the two servants who helped Aonghas Bard.

An Sgeipear — a large rocky point in the island, on which the sea breaks.

Mac Mhic-Aoidh — Murchadh Mac Shomhairle, Swainbost — the other of Aonghas Bard's helpers.

A Mhineach — the name of one of Alasdair Mac Ruairidh's cows.

Luireach — a kind of overall made of pieces of red cloth (various kinds and shades) sown together.

A WILD DAY ON RONA

Tune: I saw the brown deer and the hinds
climbing the pass together

1 On the morning of Wednesday
 I turned my face on the path to Fianuis,
 I left the lambs as was my custom;
 I did something, but I did not tend them.

2 That was a morning that was deceiving,
 I am sure that damage will happen;
 There was a man from Tolsta at that time,
 And he held on tightly.

3 The crew of the fine boat was there,
 With many of my relatives in it,
 There was Aonghas Donn and Iain Beag Mairtin,
 And the helmsman — with a ready hand.

4 I woke up early on New Year's day
 And what a dreadful sight it was,
 The white sea was all over the village
 And it was bitterly cold.

5 I did not lose my courage
 Until the water rose to the Sgitean.
 It even broke on Talamh a' Charn,
 And my children and I were in a desperate state.

6 But I was disappointed in my relatives,
 That they did not tell me about the boat
 Although it had been tied up very tightly
 I could hardly see the Sgeipear.

7 The boys went to the smithy
 Expecting that it would be warmer;
 This was when MacKay's son said:
 "My Goodness, where will I go?"

8 I went out on the path to Cro-Fhionnlaigh.
 There was n't a stone left unturned there;
 That was not what concerned me,
 I could not count the flock.

9 I had three very good lambs,
 There was a hornless lamb from the grey sheep among them,
 There was a blue-back, dark blue one
 And one of them was on the slope.

64

10   Don't you think that it's a shame
     For a man who can read English and Gaelic
     To call me a thief
     Because of the drowning in Geodha Meura?

11   You thought highly of Mineach
     If she is the best in the district.
     That night took its toll of lambs and sheep
     That would be priceless at the sales.

12   When I reach my country
     And you begin to plunder me
     And when you reach my overall
     I will give you a crown to read.

The suggestion that he was a thief may have brought Angus back to Lewis and was possibly the reason why, instead of going to Swainbost, he went out to live in a high wild place called Cuile Totair, near the edge of a steep drop to the sea on the east side of the moors at Dibidale. Kenneth was baptised at Teampull Pheadair at Swainbost, but this happened immediately on coming ashore from Rona, and the Mac-Leods probably stayed out at Cuile Totair until at least 1832, when another son, Angus, was born. Soon after this the family returned to Swainbost. Among the MacLeod children Angus became the minister at Knock, while two of his elder brothers remained in Ness, Donald living at number 18 Lionel and Kenneth at 4 Swainbost.

It was perhaps in connection with the supposed sheep stealing that a story is told about a visit made by Alexander Murray, Alasdair Mac Ruairidh, to the island.[136] He had gone out in the spring with some implements including a spade, and at a meal found the people eating one of his sheep. Out of embarrassment, they did not offer him a piece, whereupon he said, "Cha do chuiridh riamh ma' a comunn mi'", "I was never put out of a company before". Again the implication is that the system had altered and that the shepherd had no right to kill a sheep as he wished, which had been the arrangement in Kenneth MacCagie's time. It is easy to imagine why such a change would be made.

According to tradition, Aonghas Bard had more than his own family with him on Rona. There were two "servants", one of whom may have been "Mac Mhic-Aoidh", MacKay's son, and the other "fear Tholastaidh", the Tolsta man, both mentioned in the sheep-theft song. The former has also been described as "Murchadh Mac Shomhairle," Murdo, son of Samuel, in Swainbost, but it seems possible that he could have been a son of Fionnlagh Ruadh.[137] On his departure Aonghas Bard left these two men on the island for a further year to assist his successor, the man who was known as Iain Buidhe.

The MacDonalds

It is said that the "Buidhe" family came from Skye to the Lewis village of Borve in the eighteenth century, but the earliest recorded member seems to be the "Donald McOilbuy' (Dòmhnull mac Dhòmhnuill Bhuidhe) who was a tenant living at Gearinin, Knockaird, in 1718.[138] He had a son John who was tenant in 1753 and died in 1761. John's son Donald succeeded to the holding the following year; he had three sons, Donald, John (Iain Caol), and possibly Calum, father of Calum Breabadair. Both the last mentioned Donald and John were press-ganged into the army from their home at what was known as number 6 Knockaird in 1793. Within a few years the brothers came back to find that their father had been evicted from their old home and that the holding had been taken by the tacksman. Iain Caol could get no ground elsewhere in Knockaird, so he and his wife Christina Mac-Kenzie built a house at Cuile Totair high above the sea, and from there they moved to Tolsta in 1828. Donald also spent a while at Cuile Totair and then occupied a lot at number 23 Swainbost, the houses at that time being near the sea at the Druim Mòr and not far from the farm. It is supposed that the family acquired the surname of Mac-Donald in the course of the Napoleonic wars.

Donald — Dòmhnall Buidhe — married a girl from Lionel, Catherine Morrison, known as "Catrìona Chruinn", "round Kate". Over a period of nearly twenty years they had at least six children. It is sometimes claimed that the eldest was Murdo, who would have been born about 1800 at Swainbost. Murdo certainly married Mary Murray (nighean Aonghais Ruaidh) of number 13 Cross, and their first child, Donald, was born in 1825. Like many of his contemporaries, Murdo was a distiller of whisky, and was caught at least once. He went to live at number 10 Skigersta, and in the early 1830s exchanged crofts with Donald MacLean of number 7. In 1836 Murdo was drowned while fishing for ling off Skigersta, with all the rest of the crew, and nearly thirty years later his son Donald was also drowned, in the disaster called "the great drowning" (am bàthadh mòr), on 18th December 1862. After Murdo, the next child born to Dòmhnull Buidhe and Catriona Chruinn was John in 1803. There followed two more sons, Donald in 1810 and apparently a second Murdo in 1821, and three daughters, Margaret, who was born in 1805 and married Donald MacKenzie of 15 Skigersta, Mary, born in 1815, who married Alexander MacKenzie, Donald's brother, and Catherine, born in 1819.

The story of Rona continued with the second son, John, best known as "Iain Buidhe". Like his elder brother Murdo, John may have been born in Cuile Totair.[139] His father, Dòmhnall Buidhe, was

66

dead by 1825, in which year the widow Catrìona Chruinn was married again, this time to a widower called John Campbell in Port of Ness. The marriage took place on the same night as that of Catrìona's son John to John Campbell's daughter, Cirstina. John and Cirstina had their first child a year later, when a daughter Catherine was born. In 1829, before there were any other children, the family went to Rona.

Much of what survives in tradition about Rona concerns Iain Buidhe, and the island's history would have been greatly the poorer if he had not gone there. In fact it was more by chance than intention that he did go out to his lonely shepherding, since the customary arrangement which had prevailed for over a century was under review, and ideas of change were already in the air in the time of Aonghas Bard. Mr Adam, factor for the Lewis Estate, went to Rona in the summer of 1826, and reported in a letter of 6th July.[140] He had discovered that whatever peat there had once been on the island was entirely exhausted, and that the tenant was destroying the fine grassland by cutting the turf for fuel. If he had not gone to see it the grass would have been completely ruined. He suggested that a boat's crew of fishermen might be settled on Rona, with fuel sent out to them, or that the island might be abandoned to sheep. In any case the resident family would be removed. Whichever course was chosen the rent of Rona would rise almost three times, from £10 to about £30. Six fishermen would each pay a moderate sum of £5; on the other hand, an equally rewarding number of sheep would be thirty to forty, taken out to fatten for a year. Adam had found an amazingly large population of birds, and passed through a "field", almost an acre in size, of what must have been breeding gulls, sitting on their nests, almost touching each other, apparently uninterested in the visitor. He did not think of them as of much value, certainly not as useful as the gannets of Sula Sgeir, and he concluded that more might be made of carcasses salted and barrelled than of feathers. No action followed upon this report for several years, but it was a landmark in the story of Rona, since it appears to be the first sign that the owner was actually wondering what to do with the place.

The departure of John MacDonald, Iain Buidhe, to Rona, is usually associated with the distilling of whisky. According to one version, John had a still on the Swainbost machair, and used to walk with a keg of it on his back from Skigersta to Stornoway in order to sell it. On one occasion, whether at the still or on the moor, he was caught by the excise man, and was to go to prison at Dingwall for a year and a day. It was believed, however, that a man could avoid prison if he left the island for five years, a better fate than the shame of imprisonment, so John's elder brother Murdo offered to look after John's family while he spent his exile either in the Dingwall jail or in Rona.* He chose the island and went there in Alasdair Mac Ruairidh's boat. Indeed it is said that Alasdair had hidden the fugitive in the attic of the Swainbost farmhouse, in return for which help he had asked John to go to Rona, as there were few who were willing to stay there.

John's wife Cirstina would not accompany him, so his mother went with him instead. The following year, however, the boat brought out Cirstina and her daughter Catherine, and took the mother, Catrìona Chruinn, back to Ness.** Three children were born to the Mac-Donalds on Rona, Donald, Finlay and Anna, who were all baptised at Swainbost in 1835, by which time the family was obviously back in Ness. Thereafter there were further children, John, born in 1839, Murdo in 1846, Gormul or Gormelia 1848, and Norman 1850. There are many descendants of these "Buidhe" children, some of whom died in Ness within living memory. Catherine married in Shader, near Barvas, and died without a family in 1907; Finlay is said to have been born in 1834 and died on 7th April 1915; Donald who died young in 1861, married Anna Gunn, daughter of Angus Gunn, in 1851 and had four children, the first being Murdo and the second Mary, who married a descendant of Fionnlagh Ruadh; Anna married Norman MacLean from the Uig district, lived at Swainbost and died in 1913 without children; of John little is known, and Murdo, never in good health, died in 1875 aged 27; Gormul married Calum Campbell and died in Adabroc, where her grandchildren still live; Norman, born on the family croft, number 11 Cross, lived in the village all his life and died on his birthday, 11th May 1938. On the occasion of one daughter's marriage she was given a ciosan, or grass bowl, which Iain Buidhe had made on Rona. The links between the three "Rona" families must have strengthened the strong current of the island traditions running then and still in Ness.

When Iain Buidhe arrived in Rona he found the "two lads" left behind by Aonghas Bard. Perhaps "lads" is not the right word, as there is a story told about the "crusty old bachelor" and the "young lad" who served Iain Buidhe. The lad teased the old bachelor who got so angry that he would have given the boy a thrashing had not Iain Buidhe saved him. The bachelor was angered even more by this and refused to make the ewe milk cheese, a task at which he was an expert. Iain Buidhe therefore tried himself, and it is said that he was so

* An alternative version, inconsistent with the date of John's marriage, states that it was Murdo who was caught making whisky in Skigersta, and that John, as an unmarried man, took the blame and fled to Rona.
** According to one tradition, she was midwife to the children born on Rona, and married John Campbell on her return, living in Cross and then at Port, but it seems that the marriage had indeed taken place in 1825.

successful that when the cheese was sold at Dingwall or Aberdeen, it fetched "first prize". In a second story, which seems to be a different version of the first, the servants were described as two young fellows, though one was distinctly older than the other, and it was probably the younger who was described as gille-sabhal, barn-boy, to Iain Buidhe. One day, when meat was being served out at a meal, the boy complained that the elder servant got more and struck him unconscious with a meat bone. Immediately regretting his action, the boy ran out to throw himself over a cliff, but Iain Buidhe caught him round the waist and so saved him. The elder servant felt that Iain had taken the boy's part, and refused to tell him anything about how to make the cheese so Iain had to try himself. When the boat arrived Iain Buidhe reported the event to explain that the cheese might not be as good as usual but when asked what colour the cheese was he was able to say that it was the right one — a greyish green — and the cheese proved more than acceptable. The two servants came home to Ness in the boat that brought back Iain Buidhe's mother.

According to tradition, Iain Buidhe looked after seven cows and one hundred and twenty sheep on Rona, but, as will be seen later, these numbers cannot be quite accurate. He had the milk of the cows and of the ewes, and if there were twin lambs he was allowed to take one twin for winter meat. He made the ewe milk cheese, which he stored in a cool dark hut, for it was necessary to keep out as much light and air as possible. In spring he turned the feannagan, the corn and potato rigs, with a cas chrom or foot plough, and sowed the barley for which the ground was especially good. During the summer the animals were herded away from the feannagan; they were generally in the pastures enclosed with stone walls to the west at this time, but after harvest in October or even November they roamed anywhere, sheltering on Fianuis on days of southerly gales. The calves were housed in the winter. Seabirds, a valuable source of food, were summer residents only, leaving the island after the breeding season was over until their return in April or May. The birds were an unfailing supply, whereas the stock and grain were at the mercy of the seasons; in 1828 the barley was sown as usual in May, but no shower of rain touched Rona until it was cut many weeks later, and it was a poor crop.

In Iain Buidhe's time Alasdair Mac Ruairidh sent out a sgoth in September. The Ness sgoth had a keel of about twenty feet, an overall length of about thirty feet, and one sail. It apparently replaced the old galley, as was recalled years later by Murdo MacDonald, possibly John's younger brother:

"Since the large Boat failed them the Ness men have daringly often put themselves on several occasions in great danger in going to and from that island in small boats. They have been many times weather bound on Rona for 3 and on one occasion for 5 weeks, and given up as lost by their friends at home. Many a dream and g[h]ost story used to be going about concerning the Ness men while imprisoned on Rona".[141]

On the outward journey the sgoth carried supplies of oatmeal and salt for preserving fish and meat. These provisions acted as a ballast, although sometimes stones had to be added. For the return load there were the lambs not left for breeding, the barley meal, a cow or calves, and pieces of Rona sandstone which was easy to dress and round into querns for grinding the Ness barley. It is said that most of the Ness querns were made of Rona stone. The boat left Lewis from any place that was calm, Port of Ness, Stoth or Cunndal, and usually landed its cargo at Poll Thothatom or Geodha Stoth, depending on the wind and the sea, but occasionally it was necessary to use the steep-sided cleft called Sgeildige, where sheep would be taken off by lowering them down the cliff on a rope.

Although he lived until 1892, Iain Buidhe became a kind of legendary figure, possibly within his lifetime. He lived in the old house once occupied by Kenneth MacCagie, with its tunnel entrance passing between the huts where grain and cheese were stored into the long main room of the dwelling. At the upper end of this room was a bed recess, and a fire of peaty earth smouldered in the middle of the floor. Overhead were the rafters holding up the roof of turf and straw. The outside of the walls was heaped over with turf to keep out the wind and spray which could otherwise have put the fire out. Like his predecessors Iain Buidhe had no boat, but he caught fish from the rocks with great success and had the dried and salted rows hanging inside. He was big, fair-haired, and very strong; apart from carrying kegs of whisky to Stornoway he is supposed to have lifted great stones in Rona, where there was only one which he could not manage by himself, and it is said that before leaving the island he spent part of his second last day there in carrying a great stone up Leathad Fhianuis to the top, where he placed it as a mark of his stay. On one occasion he remarked on the kind of boat he would need:

"A wooden oar is no use to me, I would break it. I would need an iron oar".

He seems to have been confident that he could deal with visiting strangers. In winter, he said, there were many weeks when no-one could get ashore, and so no enemies could harm them then anyway, but in summer it was still necessary for him to hide his wife or pretend she was dead. On one such occasion the family was anxious about the presence of a ship, but ceased to worry when all the visitors did was to

70

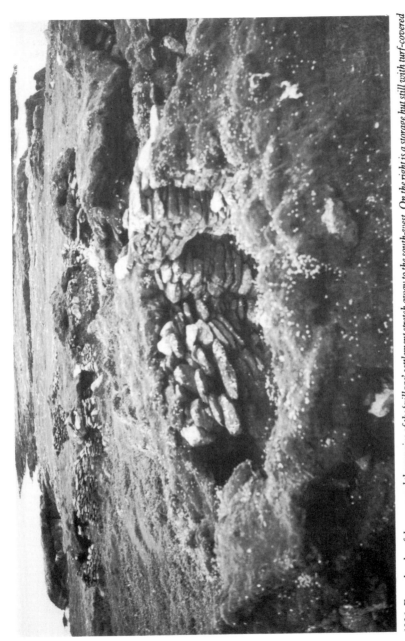

1936. From the edge of the graveyard the remains of the 'village' settlement stretch away to the south-west. On the right is a storage hut still with turf-covered roof, and further away is the inclosure understood to have been the dwelling of Iain Buidhe and his family.

(photo. Robert Atkinson)

71

give a handkerchief to the old mother Catrìona Chruinn. A ship's crew often needed fresh meat and would destroy more than they wanted by driving some sheep over the rocks. Strangers and the weather were threats to the fire, but perhaps the poor quality of the fuel presented the greatest problem. Driftwood was gathered throughout the year, dried in the summer and stored inside in the winter, but if it ran out, as it did once while John was on Rona, emergency measures might be necessary. On finding his peat fire nearly out one morning, John managed to rescue it by using a page from the Bible, a blank leaf some people say. It was of course difficult to dry clothes, and he is supposed to have kept his on, however wet they were. He never wore boots, but made sandals of sheep-skin all the time he was on the island. The other members of the family either wore the same, or, more probably, went barefoot.

Iain Buidhe grew very attached to Rona. When he was back in Ness someone remarked to him that in certain weathers he could see the island from Beinn nan Caorach, next to Beinn Dail. "I am afraid my heart would not stand it", he replied. His mind must have been filled with recollections of Rona, the noise of the kittiwakes in Slochd a' Phriosain, the gulls of Fianuis, the moaning of the seals out at Gealldruig Mor, the misty presence of the swelling ocean. Long afterwards he must have remembered the day of his leaving, when he looked back at the familiar little hills and the caverns drawing away for ever. Fifty years later in 1885 he was visited at his home in Cross by Mrs MacLeod from Port of Ness who fortunately wrote down his memories:

"I called upon the only man in Ness now living who ever lived in Rona with his family. This is what he told me . . .

"My name is John MacDonald. I am 83 years of age. I lived in Rona for five years. I brought my mother, my wife and one child to Rona with me. Three children were born to us while on the Island. We did not drink a cup of tea or coffee while on the Island nor did we miss it. We had plenty milk and home brewed ale which was excellent. We made lots of cheese from the sheeps milk. My wife went out at breakfast or dinner time and brought in as many eggs as she wanted, yes wild fowls eggs they were all eatable I assure you and as tender as hens eggs. She just had to go a few paces from the house and pick up as many as she wished for. There is excellent rock fishing in the harvest. I have seen me often for hours land as many saithe as I could bait for and haul up with the rod. The bait I used was limpets.

"I never heard of the Island of Rona being part of the glebe of Barvas, nor do I believe it, for the Church of Scotland never lost an inch of land she at any time possessed. Since the time when the Ness man threw the burning peat on Rona, the Island always belonged to the Murrays of Swainbost and Dell or Cloinne a Gow (the blacksmith's children) as they were called by us

1936. Mrs MacLeod (Bean Iain Mhurchaidh), Ocean Villa, Port of Ness, recorder of Iain Buidhe's memories and Ness correspondent of the Stornoway Gazette.

(photo. Robert Atkinson)

here. To prove this fact to you the spot where the houses were is called Ferrin a gowan, (The Blacksmiths' land.)

"The greatest number of families that were on the Island at once were six. There are ruins of *six tennants houses*. There is a churchyard. There were twelve tombstones in it when I was there. That is fifty two years ago. The church is inside of the churchyard. There is a dyke round the churchyard. Entrance by a gate. The first man who was buried in the Rona churchyard is said to be a pious man of the name of *Ronan*. Ronan lived in Oreby, a township near the Butt, and his righteous soul was vexed within him, hearing the Oreby women scolding about the pasture for their Cattle. Ronan went down to a cave to pray. He prayed that God might take him away where he would not be hearing the tongues of these wicked scolds. He went to sleep and he dreamed that God had prepared a fish to carry him away from those who vexed him, and that the fish was close to the beach. Ronan went down. There was the great whale which he saw in his dream. He got on his back, and the whale landed him safely on Rona, so named after Ronan.

"Ronan built for himself a small chapel where he used to worship often. This small sanctuary or chapel forms a part of the Church in the church-yard. When the six families were on the Island Ronan's place of worship was too small but too sacred to be destroyed.

"I never saw a rat, mouse, or any kind of vermin on the Island. It yielded excellent crops of Barley and potatoes. The Island is in size about one mile square. The stock on the Island when I was there was 200 sheep, 3 milk cows and 1 Bull. We used peats for fuel. We cut and attended to them in spring and early summer. I was very comfortable on the Island and I am sorry I left it.

"We burnt seal oil in our lamps. We killed the seals when they came on land to have their young. I will tell you as many as I can remember of the birds that breed on Rona, they are numerous. Dhu Scarve, Ian Dhu, Gillie Bric, Falk, Colk, Starnaig, Sea gulls etc etc. There are a great many others which I cannot now remember.

"I once ran the risk of coming to be without fire on the Island. This lookout was very alarming as you may imagine. There were of course no lucifer matches. When I got up in the morning early as I used to do to take a look at the sheep long before the rest of the family had time to rise, I prepared to put on a fire as usual but on passing the tongs through the peat ashes I was more than shocked to find only a small bit of live coal about as much as would light my pipe. I had not a scrap of paper on the Island except our Gaelic Bible. No time must be lost. I hurried for that precious volume and placed the small coal on the fly leaf. I hurried for a lamp and with great care I most providently got the lamp lit".[141]

In 1834 John and his family came back to Ness. Donald, only five years old, saw a horse for the first time and thought it was a strange kind of cow. Anna was about a year old, Finlay no more than a baby. They went to the croft in Swainbost which was later attached to the Free Presbyterian Manse, and lived there for a few years until a quarrel caused another move to Cross. Close by at number 45 Swainbost there lived Alexander Henderson, known locally as An Gobha Gallach, the Caithness smith. He is supposed to have come to Ness with another Caithness man, Donald Weir, about 1843, and to have been rather a wild character, although if he was it did not prevent him from eventually holding a responsible position in the district. By 1855 he was living at number 33. One day Iain Buidhe went out for a creel of peats to the stack, and found Henderson's pig snouting up his potatoes. He angrily seized the pig's back legs, swung the animal round above his shoulders and flung it down so that the neck was broken.* "In those days, it would take less than that to get the law after him", and Iain Buidhe had to move to a less good croft in Cross, which he shared with his son Finlay after Donald married and went to North Dell. The shares eventually led to a division. The rent ledger for 1855 to 1867 shows "John MacDonald" and his son Finlay at number 11, and in the final year there is a question: "Where have these tenants gone to?"[142] The answer was that they had gone to number 13, for which they were rentalled in 1868. In 1871 their rent rose by 3s to £2.15s – when they were allowed a bit of Galson Moor.[143] Within the next few years the division of number 13 was made, and in 1880 John MacDonald (Iain Buidhe) was in number 14 with Finlay in number 15, each of these described as "half of the old lot 13" and rented at £1.7s.6d.[144] The Crofters Commission reduced the sum to £1 in 1891. John's death occurred in November 1892, when his son Norman was living in the house and doing the croft work, but it was apparently Donald's son Murdo, nephew to Norman, who inherited the croft. On 15th November 1895, Murdo, who lived in North Dell, went to Galson Lodge and gave up number 14 Cross in favour of his uncle.[145]

MacLeods and MacKays again

After Iain Buidhe came home in 1834, another shepherd went to live on Rona. This was Murdo MacLeod, Murchadh Bàn mac Dhòmh-nuill, known as "am Pìobair", the Piper. Murdo, born in 1796, was a skilled and intrepid fisherman, with an uncanny knowledge of the ocean's currents and the courses they ran out from Ness. He was the discoverer of the submerged pinnacle, rising fifteen fathoms from the sea bed, called Cara Phìobair, the Piper's Rock. On one occasion,

---

* In 1866 it was noted in the rent ledger that "Henderson had his lot free for assisting the Ground Officer in matters connected with this Township and giving information regarding their stock etc . . ." Previously he had paid about 5/- or 7/6 per acre for his croft of 6.223 acres. (Lewis Estate Rent Ledgers). It is also said that the pig belonged to Ian Bàn a' Gàradh, a Morrison living in Swainbost next to no. 1 Habost and next to Iain Buidhe, and that the quarrel was between them.

when some nets had been lost, Murdo was asked to find them. He was then an old man and had to be taken in a cart to Port, where he was lifted into the boat and put near the tiller so that he could give directions how to track the nets. After sailing for a good while, Murdo said "There should be a buoy now", and there it was.

Murdo's father moved from the Point district to Gress, and Murdo himself was one of those who came from Gress to settle in North Dell at Baile Griais, the Gress township. He took his family out to Rona, but they stayed only a year or perhaps less.* This shorter period was not a planned arrangement, but was the consequence of a sad accident, when one of Murdo's sons fell to his death over the western rocks somewhere between Sgeildige and Lòba Sgeir. It is said that the body lay on a ledge visible but inaccessible, decaying in the sun and rains. The family could stay on the island no longer, and returned with the tenant's boat to Ness, and after living again for a while in North Dell, the MacLeods moved first to number 25 and then to number 28 Cross, where descendants still are. There are also descendants of Murdo's son John still in North Dell.

Murdo's wife was Mary Graham of Back. Four sons were born before the family went to Rona, Norman in 1824, Alexander in 1829, Donald and John in 1833. The last two were born in Back but baptised in North Dell, which shows that the move was also in 1833. It is not known which son it was who was killed in the island. Both Norman and Donald later went to stay from time to time on Rona. Apparently three more children were born after the return to Ness, when Murdo and his sons made up the crew of their own fishing boat and spent days and nights in the ocean off the Butt.

It would not have been surprising if the disaster that overtook the MacLeod family had marked the end of the shepherd line on Rona, but it did not. Perhaps because Alasdair Mac Ruairidh was still tenant or because of the strength of tradition the old arrangement was not abandoned, and yet another family left for the island, probably in 1836. The man was already familiar with Rona, for he had been born there, although he had left when only about five years old. He was Malcolm MacKay, son of Fionnlagh Ruadh, and living at number 6/7 Fivepenny to which he had probably come about 1830 when seven new lots were made. He was married to Catherine Murray, who was about seven years older than her husband and lived another thirty years after his death. They had four children, of whom the youngest, John, married Ann MacDonald (nighean Dhòmhnuill Bhuidhe) of number 37 Tolsta and so, as often happened, two Rona families were again linked. Not much is known of Malcolm's stay on Rona except

* According to family tradition the period was February to August.

that at least his son Donald was born on the island and possibly also the youngest son John. After returning the family lived again at Fivepenny. Malcolm was a fisherman, and he and all the crew of the *sgoth* were drowned off the Butt in 1839.* In 1880 John, known as Iain Donn, and his brother Donald divided the croft at Fivepenny, John occupying number 6 until he emigrated to Quebec five years later. When he came back he lived as a cottar on the croft, which had been combined again by Donald. About 1860 Donald married Margaret Gunn (nighean Iain 'ic Alasdair) of number 20 Lionel, and they had five children, of whom the youngest was Jessie who married her second cousin Donald MacKay of number 14 Skigersta. Donald lived on until he was eighty, dying in 1916. He, or possibly John, was probably the last to be born in Rona, as there seems to have been no further family on the island.

The King of Rona and the Piper

From about 1840 onwards Rona might be considered a deserted island, although it was not given up to the sea-birds and the seals. Crops and cattle could no longer be raised there on a regular basis, but sheep continued to graze the rich pastures and birds were hunted from time to time. Human occupation became haphazard and occasional, and it is not clear what arrangements were made for people to go out. In 1841 there were three young men, described as male farm servants, on the island when the census was taken; they were Alan Campbell, son of Aonghas Og in Swainbost and later in Lionel, Norman MacRitchie, son of Colin MacRitchie in Habost, and Murdo MacDonald, who could possible have been the younger brother of Iain Buidhe. All were said to be eighteen years old, but if he was indeed of the "Buidhe" family, Murdo ought to have been twenty. Ten years later, in 1852, Alan Campbell and his family emigrated, probably to Megantic, near Quebec. Norman MacRitchie, married and living in Swainbost, emigrated at the same time; it is possible that his father, Colin, was related to Kenneth MacRitchie (MacCagie) as the two families were the only MacRitchies in Habost.

These three men might not have stayed in Rona for more than a summer and perhaps not even as long as that, but it appears that the next recorded inhabitant, Donald MacLeod, whose stories have already been quoted, did live there for a full year, probably as a shepherd. It was clearly a time when the owner, Sir James Matheson, who bought the Lewis Estate in 1844, was uncertain what to do with his remote possession. From what he said later, Donald MacLeod did

* The sgoth, Eathar Challuim mac Fhionnlaigh, is said to have been the first boat lost in Ness.

not much enjoy his stay, possibly because he was on his own. According to a report of October 1850,

"Donald MacLeod *King of Rona* was its last human inhabitant.* He resided there about 6 years ago for a period of 12 months — he appears to have been weary of his solitude and expresses a horror at the idea of being left there again. His residence in Rona, together with his rude yet muscular figure, have procured him the above title".[146]

It seems unlikely that Donald was one of the Piper family. Most probably he was Dòmhnull Ruadh, who was born in 1791, lived for a while at Swainbost, and died in the 1850s. This Donald was married to Ann Morrison and had eight children, all born in Swainbost, among them Finlay, born in 1821, and Roderick, born in 1831. By 1841 they were living at number 22 Cross, although a son, Norman, nicknamed Tohan, was at number 1 Cross, a croft with the house then on the old village site towards the sea called Cnoc Eogaidh. In tradition, Dòmhnull Ruadh was the man who assisted the "sappers" of the Ordnance Survey, and received his title of "King of Rona" because "he was a braggart and thought he owned everything".

The only other occasional residents of Rona known after Donald MacLeod, were Donald and Norman of the Piper's family, and of these two, only Norman features much in tradition and record. Norman MacLeod, usually called Tormod Pìobar, used to go out to Rona for both winter and summer seasons when he was a middle-aged man in his forties and fifties.** He built himself a stone "beehive" hut on Fianuis, known as Both Thormoid Phìobair, and looked after sheep on the island. In the early 1880s he had about 100 sheep there himself for which he paid £30 rent to the absentee Daniel Murray. In 1885 it was remarked that Rona was capable of pasturing about 200 sheep:

"Prior to being so let it seems to have been occupied by several families of crofters the last of whom left the Island a long time ago. Since the departure of the crofters and the occupancy of the Island by sheep it has been necessary to keep a Shepherd or Shepherds on the Island during the winter to look after the sheep. This duty was, prior to the summer of 1884, performed by one man who resided alone on the Island every winter and only visited Lewis in summer to see his family. He was popularly known as the 'King of Rona'."[147]

This lonely shepherd, who had apparently inherited Donald MacLeod's title as well as his job, was Norman MacLeod. His feelings about Rona were evidently different from Donald's; it is said that,

* Earlier in the report he was called "(commonly styled 'King of Rona')".
** Traditionally he is known to have been there several times in summer to clip the sheep.

78

when he went once on a visit to fetch sheep, he could hardly be persuaded back into the boat.

With Norman MacLeod, Tormod Pìobair, there ends the history of Rona's people, although of course a dwindling number of those born on the island, and a larger company of those who had stayed there for a while, lived among the villages of Ness. On 1st December 1885 Mrs MacLeod, of Port, wrote that information on Rona could be easily collected "as there are a great many men at Ness who lived in Rona in the Murrays' time".[148] In the same year Murdo MacDonald, perhaps the same Murdo as was on Rona in 1841, remembered what he had learned about the island:

> "There were in my young days 50 years ago 4 families in our parish (Ness) who had resided on the island of Rona, some of them for upwards of 20 years. They were leaving the island as the young people were growing up. I mind that those who were born and brought up on the island were stout plump or heavy mostly of a fair complexion but not so active as other people. They used to give us most thrilling accounts of sufferings endured in stormy winters. Snow did not remain long on the island but during gales and heavy sea the spray covered the whole of the island. Their fires were several times put out".

At the end of his account, Murdo wrote:

> "Such then is all I recollect about Rona stories unless I were to go again among the Ness people to refresh my memory".[149]

PART III

VISITORS' DAYS

The Ordnance Survey and T. S. Muir

In summer, when journeys over the ocean can be more safely made, Rona is a green island, with its long southern slope of rich grass facing the sun and the warmer breeze. To fishermen at such a time it is a pleasant, welcoming place, as it must have been to the holy men and Vikings long ago, and certainly was to Malcolm Stewart, visiting in 1930. "No one", he said, "could ever fail to experience immense pleasure on first landing on North Rona".[150] Perhaps part of this pleasure is relief on stepping ashore after a long, rough sea voyage. Yet nearly everyone who has been on Rona in summer has been impressed with its fertility, the rich growth of grass and, formerly, the long waving corn. Great crowds of sea birds fill the cliffs and spread over the tops of the promontories, with their endless crying making loud the spring and summer air. Seal heads bounce in the surf and swell, and everywhere there is busy movement. For half the year Rona is a concentration of life and activity.

If he landed at Geodha Stoth in the season of birds and flowers, St. Ronan might have thought himself fortunate to have reached such an island, and undoubtedly there were good reasons for people to go and live there. Those who wished or were compelled to settle however had no easy task in reaching Rona, and the dangers of the voyage kept many from making it. Even if begun in calm, the journey could soon become perilous, with rapid changes of the weather, surging seas, and a landing almost impossible if the wind was at all easterly. But there were days when, whether from Ness, Sutherland or the Orkneys, a boat could reach Rona without much trouble, and come in close to the rocks of Geodha Stoth.

Stoth came to be considered "the largest and most commodious bay", affording "an excellent landing place",[151] and in a rock there was fixed in more recent time an iron mooring ring. If it was impossible to get ashore there the boat could move round to the opposite side of Fianuis, at the narrow deep creek called "Skildaga" or "Sgeildige", where it was necessary to climb up a steep cliff. Failing this, a landing might be tried at Poll Thothatom or Poll Heallair on the south shore, the former being reckoned the safest landing place after Geodha Stoth. But the safety and suitability of any spot depended entirely on the state of the wind and sea.

To add to the hazards, there were reefs all round the coast, in particular "Bogha Mheadhoin là", the Mid-day Rock, a small reef visible only at low water of spring tides and "very dangerous for vessels".[152] There were also the Gealldruig rocks, lying further out; Gealldruig Beag showed only at low water, and Gealldruig Mòr, beloved of seals, was usually beset with a heavy swell. To reach Rona

The fishing boat 'Sandy Bay', from Tolsta, is off Sgeildige because the usual landing place at Geodha Stoth could not be approached owing to bad weather.

(photo. Swainbost Farm Collection)

at all demanded skilled seamanship as well as good fortune.

On 1st September 1846, Henry Otter, Captain on board the "Sparrow", reported that he could discover no water on Rona.[153] He found the island well covered with grass but could not imagine how people had survived there. Water there was, however, in the several wells, although in a dry summer it ran short and tasted very salty, and in many parts of the island rain left pools in rocks and hollows, sufficient for cattle and sheep to drink and breeding seals to flounder in. It was possible to live on Rona, and even to flourish, but only at a mean level of continual risk and frequent hardship. As a place to visit, however, to call in at for a while, the island had many attractions. There were its green appearance, its varied produce, and its unusual human residents; and after the people had gone visitors came especially to see what traces of occupation were left.

Over the centuries many kinds of ship must have approached Rona. Viking longboats, travellers' yachts, seine netters and warships, all have found the island slowly coming into view out of the sea haze, have measured distances and fixed positions, and have run for shelter in the lea of Fianuis on a wild evening with the wind rising.

One of the earlier and stranger stories involved pirates.[154] In July 1615 the Privy Council of Scotland was concerned with the subject of

83

pirates, some of whom were brought to trial. It was reported on 4th July that a certain Captain Mason of Lyne, with five or six others in his company, was warded within the Tolbooth of Edinburgh "upon very probable suspitiones of Pirracye". Some four years previously Mason had purchased a lease of the "Assyse-hering" (i.e. herring) of the "North Isles" and on a visit there he had met with his acquaintance, the Bishop of the Isles, Andrew Knox, whom he transported to and from Ireland. In April 1612, presumably in return for the favour, he secured from the Bishop a lease of "a lytle Ylle, called Rona", but until 1615 he never "com to tak possession of the Ylle, nor to try the worth thairof". Mason had a "pretty bark", and when sailing in it to the Isles he took on board at Yarmouth one Captain Wilman, who had been a notable pirate but had been granted the King's pardon. There were two others along with Wilman. Then, in a pretence of going to Rona to take possession and try the fishing there, though no salt barrels, fishing tackle or "victuallis" were on board, Mason and Wilman went to Orkney where two more were added to the crew, one as cook, the other as pilot. They then made off for Rona, but the winds being "contrarious" and the captain "not daring tae land there", they continued to Mull where they spent four days. While there Mason offered to help MacLean of Duart to pursue some rebels of Islay in the hope of receiving a reward from the King. Accordingly MacLean fitted him up with supplies, but Mason sailed back towards Rona where he stayed half a day — whether ashore or on board is not certain. He then returned to Orkney, raised the number of his crew to seventeen, and moved on up to Shetland and across to the coast of Norway. Here, after lying in wait in "a bay under a craig", he plundered a ship from Copenhagen. When apprehended Mason tried to convince his captors that Wilman had stirred up a mutiny and taken over the ship, and so was really to blame for the piracy. Nothing further seems to have been recorded of this unlikely visit to Rona.

Detachments of men or whole crews have from time to time come ashore to find out what was on the island. On 24th July 1813, H.M.S. Fortunée and H.M.S. Dauntless came in sight of Rona as they cruised protectively off Scotland's northwest coast in search of the American frigate "President", and on the following day Fortunée hove to and sounded in sixty fathoms. A boat was sent ashore for information, no doubt given by an apprehensive Kenneth MacCagie, and when it returned at 5 o'clock in the afternoon the ship sailed away. For a week and more Fortunée and Dauntless took bearings between Sula Sgeir and the Orkneys, during which time several merchant ships were chased, boarded, searched and released.[155] Such activity in the midst of the ocean must have been often watched curiously and fearfully by the people living on Rona.

Parties coming ashore caused more urgent concern, as the stories show. The members of one family living on the island in the early nineteenth century recollected such an episode and spoke of it many times:

> "A warship anchored off the island early on the day. A boat put off from the ship with 12 men and 2 officers, all armed. When the man in charge (of the island) saw so many men leaving the ship he took to the other side of the island with his wife and two daughters and lowered them down 50 fathom over the cliff into a cave with food to last them for a week. He then met the boat at the landing place and escorted them over the island. When returning to the house one of the officers spoke in Gaelic, asking as to how they got on in such a place and how they employed their time. He wanted to see the butter and cheese they made. The man told them to take a cheese and divide it amongst them which seemed to please them well. The officer offered to buy some. The man told him it was not his to sell, whereupon he ordered two of his men into the cheese house and to pick out 21 of the largest. He offered a guinea for them. The man would not take the money out of his hand. The officer threw it down on the ground saying to the man that he was an impudent little man. The officer next ordered his men to take 8 of the best sheep they could find which they did. He offered the man another guinea which was also refused. [The] officer next selected the best heifer on the island. The little man got outrageous when he was offered another guinea and when the officer presented his gun at the heifer the man stepped in before the muzzle saying that he would be dead before he would suffer any more robbery of what was entrusted to him.
>
> "[The] officer held back his gun saying 'you are the most courageous impudent little man that I ever met and for your courage and your zeal for your master's property I will leave you your heifer'."[156]

This warship, supposed to be a French man 'o war, was one of many which sought to plunder the island. A story told about 1840 described how five men landed one day from a ship, and how one of them insulted or tried to kiss one of the young women that they found there. Resenting the familiarity and being no weakling, she threw the sailor to the ground. He made a second attempt, with the same result. In his anger the man struck the girl, and one of her brothers intervened. A fight began, and the sailor received a blow on the head which killed him. His companions made for the boat, leaving their mate to be buried on the island. "That happened", said the storyteller, "as near as I can guess 100 years ago. Ever since then families on the island took the precaution to hide the women whenever strangers attempted to land there".[157]

The landing of strangers suggested trouble since it was impossible to tell why they had come. Sometimes they came only to mock the islanders, as in the case of more "pirates", who made their way up to a house and deliberately put out the fire by throwing water over it.

Nothing could be more disastrous for the inhabitants who no doubt marvelled to see it re-lit with tinder and "two white stones". Whatever his motives, however, the stranger was certainly as curious to make the acquaintance of those who lived so remotely as they were cautious of meeting him, and through the centuries the same scene was enacted many times, in which those at sea gazed wonderingly at the island getting slowly nearer and those on shore watched with equal intentness the approach of the distant ship.

After Dòmhnull Ruadh's return to Ness, Rona was, for most of the time, deserted, and there were no inhabitants to be frightened by visiting strangers. Sheep were left there, and had to be attended to from time to time, but no-one occupied a house in the old village and the buildings fell in and decayed under the rains and wind.

Then in the autumn of 1846, the Ordnance Survey appeared for the first time in the Western Isles, preparing their new maps which were to be issued along with sea charts from the Hydrographic Survey. From 14th to 16th October 1850, Second Corporal Michael Hayes was out at Rona, surveying the island and taking down, as best he could, the names of cliffs and creeks and other prominent features from the same Donald MacLeod, "King of Rona". Other informants were John Morrison, Donald MacRae, and John MacKay, the last being possibly that Iain MacKay, son of Fionnlagh Ruadh, who went to Rona again with T.S. Muir in 1857 and told him what he believed the surveyors had done to the roof of the cell. The main problem for Hayes was that he did not understand much Gaelic and probably knew nothing about Norse names, so that what he wrote down in his notebook was not always recognisable. Twenty years later Alexander Carmichael, who checked names in Harris and elsewhere for the Survey, explained the faults of the method:

> "The system pursued by the Ordnance Survey in regard to taking up place names is altogether erroneous. Non-Gaelic speaking men go about among non-English speaking people to take down Norse-Gaelic names with their English meanings! These lists then are sent to the district office at Inverness or to the head office Southampton in each of which there is a Gaelic writer who is expected to write out the names correctly. And finally the lists are sent down to the 'local authority' who is asked but is 'not expected to do more than give his opinion' of this precious nonsense and roundabout work".[158]*

What served to confuse the issue even further was that the various local informants did not always agree about a name, so that sometimes Hayes had to record several versions. Donald MacLeod commonly differed from the other three, as with the name of the usual landing,

* It is said that Iain Buidhe's son, Iain, helped the Ordnance Survey in the Stornoway-Barvas area.

for which his was rendered "Geodh Sthu", while the others were united in "Geodh a Stoth". The surveyor's notebook suggests that MacLeod and Morrison were more accurate than the other two, since their versions related more closely to names that occur in other records. For the deep gully on the northwest side of the Tòbha MacKay and MacRae supplied "Geodha Mairi", which, being simply if loosely translated as "Mary's Creek", appeared eventually on the map, but MacLeod gave "Geodh Maire" and Morrison "Geodha Meire", and these versions treated as one correspond to the name as it appears in tradition or in Aonghas Bard's poem. In the end, therefore, Hayes' record of Donald MacLeod's information may be closer to the original than the words that appeared on the published map.[159]

On 17th October 1850 Miles Carbery took over from Hayes, and after spending the day at Rona continued to Sula Sgeir with Donald MacLeod. By early 1852 the reports of both Hayes and Carbery had been tidied up by Captain Burnaby, who signed his name to accounts they had provided of the two islands, and who has since been generally held to be their author. T.S. Muir was the first to publish Burnaby's description of Rona, and gives the date of it as 3rd February 1852.[160] This description provides some details of the appearance of the island, with its rugged shores, two hills, good soil and "beautifully green" pasture — "indeed the whole Island, with the exception of about 50 acres, may be considered arable land interspersed with a few small rocks and numerous small piles of stones." Even only six years or so after Donald MacLeod's residence on Rona it was possible to look upon the buildings and other traces of occupation as "evidence" of a life that, having continued for centuries almost without written record, had now ended except in the memories of a dwindling company of Ness people. The surveyors, like the visitors of future times, had to guess what the walls and "piles of stones" signified, and their report shows just how quickly the world of the Rona families was vanishing away:

"A small portion on the Southern side appears to have been cultivated, and has it is said yielded excellent Barley. It is now rented by a farmer from Lewis as a sheep farm and it feeds about 200 sheep at present. There are five or six rude, flat-roofed ruinous huts on it, the neatest and smallest of which is said to have been a church. There is also a graveyard here in which there is a rude stone Cross without any inscription. There are neither Rats nor Mice, and but very few Birds on it. It has no peat moss and not much sea weed. There is a sufficiency of Spring water on its southern shore.

"Seals are very numerous here but not easily killed, and Codfish abound around its Coast."[161]

The large number of seals and the lack of birds are what might be expected in the autumn season, when seals come in to breed and the

Leaving Geodha Stoth for the fishing boat.

summer bird population has left for the open sea. The surveyors also noted good landing places together with important wind directions but shelter was limited and the occasion, six years before, when three vessels anchored together off Geodha Stoth, was described as entirely exceptional. "Articles of any weight", it was observed, "may be safely landed at Rona providing the weather is moderate, but the small Boat, which must be used on such a duty, should invariably be drawn up on the shore after use, and for this purpose ten men will be sufficient for a boat of 24 feet Keel".[162]

Through the efforts of the surveyors, whose presence and work he had done much to instigate in the first place, Sir James Matheson, owner of Rona, became aware of the island's virtues as a remote yet habitable place. The idea dawned that perhaps a sort of natural prison would be more worthwhile than continued grazing for 200 sheep. An early version of the Ordnance Survey's map of the island was prepared, with a heading that included the words: "Island of North Rona . . . a dependency of the Lews . . . Proposed as a Penal Settlement".

The distances to the island from the Butt of Lewis and from Cape Wrath gave an indication of where Rona was and of its attractive remoteness. On the map of "Rhona" itself there were two or three English placenames, and some wells, walls and, between Poll Heallair and Poll Thothatom, "Small Enclosures" were marked. Accompanying the map the Burnaby report of 1852 suitably noted the case of the Ness woman transported to Rona, the "horror" which the "King of Rona" felt at the idea of going back there, and the additional possibilities of Sula Sgeir as the place to which a man had been transported from Rona for sheep-stealing. Attached to the report were appropriate quotations from MacCulloch on the ability of the island to support people and on its extreme isolation, together with four "considerations" which were "suggested in recommendation of the plan":

1 "The large saving of the expense of transportation to Australia or any other distant Colony".
2 "The facility of guarding the convicts in Rona, from its having only three landing-places, two of which are difficult of access; while the rest of the Island is surrounded by high cliffs, more or less abrupt".
3 "The means of out-door employment to the convicts in cultivating the ground, in addition to the usual in-door occupations of a penitentiary".
4 "While the attractions of transportation to Australia, etc. operate in some degree as a premium to crime, more especially since the discovery of the Gold regions, it is thought that the dreary prospect of passing some joyless years in the midst of the stormy billows of the North Sea [i.e. North Atlantic] would tend much more to deter from crime, and from its sobering effect on the mind, would afford a better chance of reclaiming the guilty from their vicious habits".

The papers were intended to promote a proposal that Sir James Matheson had already made. He would "give up Rona to the Government, as a Penal Settlement", presumably in return for financial or other rewards. It is not clear who was responsible for adding the "considerations" and quotations to the foot of the Burnaby report, but the extra paragraphs were dated "London March 3, 1852".[163] Whatever response they received, the plan came to nothing.

Their work in the area finished, the surveyors moved on, leaving Rona to the fishermen, and the crew of an occasional sgoth up from Ness for sheep. In the summer-time cargo ships were more frequent round the Hebrides, and, in July 1857, the "Ada", a small trading sloop, brought salt to Ness for the fishing season. It happened that T.S. Muir, an Edinburgh antiquarian interested in the sites and remains of ancient Scottish churches, came to explore the west coast during the 1850s, and in the summer of 1857 made an arrangement with the "Ada" for a voyage out to Rona, which he called "this wildly-surrounded and now humanly-abandoned spot".[164] Thus on the day appointed Muir was in Port of Ness, "down at Tota Gormaig with the gneiss and the mushrooms, and then, at a jump, on board the Ada", urging the skipper to unload the salt more quickly onto the old Port quay.[165]

Muir had long heard of Rona and knowing the Ordnance party had been there a few years before he had read Captain Burnaby's account. This, together with the excitement he already felt in visiting the little islands, made him eager to get there, more eager than he ever was to reach anywhere else. On the green cliff edges of Ness, he said,

> "The mind's eye gets troubled with visions of *"ane little isle, lying towards the north northeist from Lewis, three score miles of sea, callit Ronay."*
>
> "O these endless little isles! and of all little isles, this Ronay! Yet, much as hath been seen, not to see *thee*, lying clad with soft verdure, and in thine awful solitude, afar off in the lap of wild ocean, — not to see thee with the carnal eye, will be to have seen nothing!
>
> "Yet, three score miles — rocks — surge — uninhabited — uncouth landing places: how to get to it — and upon it, — that is a question!"[166]

Now Muir had found an answer to the question and in fine weather and a favourable wind, he and the man he called "my pilot", Iain MacKay, journeyed in the sloop Ada into the "awful solitude" of the ocean.

Towards evening the vessel came round the Tòbha and hove to off Geodha Stoth. Muir and his pilot landed by a dinghy without difficulty, Iain MacKay tying the mooring rope round a large stone, and then they set off up Leathad Fhianuis and over to the silent desolate ruins of the village. Muir found the "low stone-covered passages" still mostly complete, though the houses were roofless and empty save for the odd quern stone lying about. After looking for the house in which he had lived when a boy, Iain took his companion to the chapel and cell, where he helped him in measuring the buildings. Suddenly "taking fright about the boat", Iain hurried away, and Muir was left to finish the task himself, but nervous at being on his own and with the night coming on, he abandoned the "very imperfect inspection of my object" and ran down to the shore where, much to his relief, he found the boat safe "and Iain quietly sitting by it smoking his pipe".[167]

An hour ashore was hardly sufficient to make sketches of the chapel, never mind take note of the rest of the village and island, but at first Muir seemed to have no wish to return. "Whilst looking back", he wrote, "from the deck of the *Ada* with something like affectionate regret upon Rona, as it gradually disappeared in the distance and gloom, it did not occur to me that I should ever desire to see it again".[168] In the course of their later conversation, however, Iain MacKay told Muir that on their next visit he would see more. "I'll shew you all about — all the queer places, and the birds: we'll do all that, when you come next year".[169] The following year Muir was at the Loch Roag islands and at the Flannans, but he did eventually decide to return to Rona, "a longing to know it more perfectly than I did, took me back, conditioned for a stay longer than was that of my first flighty visit".[170]

It was in fact three years before Muir made his second journey to the island. This time he had found different transport:

"Informed that Mr Daniel Murray, of Dell, was preparing for his annual wool-gathering trip . . . matters were so assorted that he and I, together, left the Butt in the *Hawk*, a nice little yacht, which had come round for us from Stornoway".[171]

Muir was accompanied by a Stornoway schoolmaster, who wanted to enjoy a few days' holiday and some cormorant shooting, and again Iain MacKay, who was no doubt ready to be a guide.[172] As they approached the Tòbha, they saw in Geodha Stoth one of the two boats Murray had sent out the evening before with crews of sheep-gatherers and clippers. The boat made towards them, and took aboard the visitors with the intention of putting them ashore. The swell was rising, however, and landing at Geodha Stoth proved impossible, so they had to row round the tip of Fianuis and in to the "hideously caverned" Sgeildige, "where, after a few minutes' fun, we all got safely landed". The "fun" involved "leaping singly out as the boat rose time after time to the edge of a shelf in the cliff".[173] They then climbed up onto Fianuis, where, at the foot of the slope leading to the rest of the island they saw the fold or "fank" where the clipping was to take place. As it was late they would have liked to have spent the night there but the boats were being hauled out at the south-western point near Sceapull, and Murray thought the party should all be there too, so they struggled across to a "very rugged but sheltered spot" beside Caolas Lòba Sgeir, where "a glowing peat fire was got up to cook the supper, and make our wild resting-place for the night look as homely as possible". Daniel Murray made up a bed for Muir out of one sail, and a sort of tent with another by stretching it over an oar. Muir could not sleep, and lay listening to the snores of his friends "and watching the spectre-like shapes of the rocks, which seemed to dance, go, and come, with every fall and flash of the fire". Further off there was the heaving roar of the sea along Leac na Sgròb, the distant seals of Gealldruig Mòr, and perhaps the sharp twitter of a fork-tailed petrel as it darted through the night around them.

At dawn everybody had breakfast, after which Murray and his men went off to deal with the sheep while Muir and the schoolmaster were left to finish their food and amuse themselves. The day turned out calm and sunny, so first they explored the island by strolling along the cliff edges of Tòn Breighe and so down to Fianuis, a walk that was "about the most pleasureable I have ever experienced". They then separated for a time, the schoolmaster going off to shoot his birds, Muir to the village and the chapel, until they happened to meet again at some point of the coast to which each had wandered.

> "Heartily worn out with the incessant rambling and the heat of the sun . . . we lay down for a rest, but the passing of time, and thoughts of how our friends on the other side might be getting through with the clip, put us soon straight on the way thither to learn what was doing . . .
> "On making the plain, we found there was yet a good deal to do, as the sheep, which had to be collected without the assistance of dogs, were every now and then breaking over the *crò*, so that the men were compelled to be constantly going off in pursuit of them all over the island".

By early evening most of the work was done, and a tired Daniel Murray decided to leave the remainder for the crews of the boats to complete. Muir and his friend, with a boy from the yacht, crossed to collect the miscellaneous pots and other things from Sceapull, and carry them back over to Geodha Stoth, where, on their arrival, they found Murray ready to embark and Iain MacKay "encaved with his boat to lift us out to the *Hawk*". So they went aboard, and in a glorious sunset began a slow calm voyage over to Sula Sgeir which took until early next morning. A good part of a second fine day was spent there among the gannets, and then the Hawk sailed back to Port of Ness, which was reached on the sunny evening of Thursday 12th July 1860.

The Deserted Island

Muir and his friends, and the surveyors before them, were the first of the "modern" visitors. They found the island abandoned as a place to live and as yet undisturbed by naturalists and people of their own kind. For them the ruined Rona village could still bring the world of Fionnlagh Ruadh or Iain Buidhe to life, for among the tumbled stones still lay the lamps, grindstones and other remnants of daily existence in times gone for ever.

The "village" they saw, and which can still be seen, was of unknown age.

Furthest up the slope stood the cell and the chapel weathering into ruin, with the slight mound of an ancient enclosing wall or earth dyke fitting closely around them. At its eastern edge, about fifteen feet

1935. The west gable wall (now fallen) of the chapel, with the Tobha and its cairns rising beyond the inner cleft of Poll Thothatom. Below the chapel to the right are the ruined walls of the eastmost inclosure.

(photo. Robert Atkinson)

from the cell, this mound merged into an oval-shaped enclosure with a square or rectangular form inside containing a heap of loose stones, perhaps all that remained of Teampull Mhionagain or Teampull nam Manach. On its east and south sides the mound also met the much larger enclosing wall which surrounded the graveyard, and which in some parts had fallen down to the slopes outside, although the entrance was still well preserved. The uneven surface of the ground within the graveyard north of the chapel suggested that other structures might have stood there, and scattered among the thick grass were the rough simple tombstones.

Three groups of buildings, including houses and huts, were not far away, one southeast of the chapel, one partly merged with the graveyard wall, and the third lying a little further off to the southwest. These seemed to be the three "inclosures" composing "the little village" to which the Reverend Donald Morison had been taken late in the seventeenth century. At that time there was a population of about thirty, in five families, so that it appears that in at least one inclosure there was more than one tenant. Each tenant had a dwelling, barn, byre, store and a porch on each side of the door; the walls were dry stone and the roofs were thatched. The appearance of an inclosure was unusual, even to a Ness man, and when the MacLeods were shipwrecked there they found what they called "a kind of a House", a phrase which suggests that the dwelling was different from the normal habitations in Lewis or Harris. After the starvation and drowning around 1700 only one dwelling was needed for the single families on the island, and they apparently occupied the southwest "inclosure", while the other two fell into disrepair. MacCulloch found Kenneth MacCagie and his family living in what appeared from the outside to be a green hillock. Within, under the sheltering cover of thatch and turf, and "excavated in the earth", were the living room with its bed pits, and the various stores, barns and so on, the whole being acccessible through the long twisting passage from the low door. This same dwelling was inhabited by Iain Buidhe, and the few others that came after him; it is still complete enough for its former appearance to be imagined.

There were also at least two separate buildings in the village standing apart from the three "inclosures". One was small, oval, and still had its roof of stone slabs covered with turf, just like a cleit — store-hut — on St. Kilda. West of the southwest "inclosure" was a ruin that looked a bit like a small Lewis thatched house, quite different in style and probably of more recent date. In its eastern side there was a door and a window, while the northern part of the interior from the door back to the end wall was occupied by a grass grown platform. The building was a kiln, important for the drying of the

The ath *or kiln building with doorway and small window from the south-west inclosure.*
(photo. Author's Collection)

A makeshift fireplace and the remains of a meal uncovered in the basin of the kiln.
(photo. Author's Collection)

grain before grinding; the kiln pit was in the middle of the platform, with the fire tunnel dipping down through the west wall to emerge at ground level on the outside.

Further west still, some yards from the village buildings, was a group of six small "folds" enclosed with the tumbled stones of low walls, and in the middle the remains of three huts. In 1850 the place consisted of:

> "The ruin of a hut, with three large, and the same number of small enclosures. Most of the walls of the former are still standing — they are about four feet high and composed of Stone and Earth. The fences of the latter are built of stone and are about two feet high. They appear to be very old".[174]

The name given to this area by Donald MacLeod was noted as "Crò Eoin Cheannich", but the version preferred by the others, and which appeared on the map, was "Cro Iain Mhic Choinnich". Whether the fold was called after John the merchant or John, son of Kenneth, may never be known for certain, but the former does seem possible. A low part of the shore nearby, described in 1850 as "a creek or indentation . . . in which a landing may be effected in very fine weather with a Southerly wind", was called "Cladach Crò Iain Dheirg", shore of Iain Dearg's fold.

These folds were only some of many ruined structures outside the village itself and the walls of its surrounding fields. Down at Sceapull was a small patch of arable with "three small enclosures on it, the fences of which are built of stone and about two feet in height". Close by was the mound of Buaile na Sgrath, said to mean "Turf Park" because from there "the inhabitants of Rona took the Sods . . . for the purpose of roofing their houses"; it was arable ground "and has two enclosures on it, one on the N. and another on the S. side".[175] Mounds of loose stones, some of them turf covered, were to be seen in many places, in lines east of the village before the slope up the Tòbha, and west of the village also, the larger being possibly the ruins of storage huts. Those in lines below the Tòbha were joined by stone walls, and up the Tòbha itself were further piles of stones and the traces of walls running across the hill. A prominent rocky hillock between the Tòbha and the steep slope down to Fianuis was called "Sithean a Croer" by Donald MacLeod; the surveyors found it to be "A small green hill . . . which has a small hill of stones and a few enclosures on it".[176] Not much trace was left of the enclosures, but there were two or three with perhaps a small hut.

At the foot of Leathad Fhianuis was the rectangular sheep fold, commonly known in more recent times as the fank, and it is possible, though unlikely, that it was the pen of which MacCulloch wrote: "The

1947. The ridge of Rona from the north-east, with the Tobha to the left, the rocky knoll of 'Sithean a Croer' and the sea shining below Geodha Meadhar.

(photo. Robert Atkinson)

shepherd informed us that his sheep fold, which seemed secure enough to our eyes, was often washed away."[177] A general description of "Feenish" was given by the surveyors:

"The Northern end of Rona, which is enclosed on the Southern side by a fence which runs from Skildiga to Geodh Sthu. The Northern half of this portion is bare rock, without a particle of vegetation. The surface of the Southern portion consists of good green pasture and has numerous enclosures, piles and a few shealings in ruins scattered over it. There is none of it more than a 100 feet above the level of the Sea".[178]

The "fence" or wall ran across near the fank. The enclosures to the north of it were vaguely set out with rough lines of stones, into which were built here and there some huts with corbelled roofs, one of them being known later as "Both Thormoid Phìobair", after the man who used it and perhaps made it. Towards the northern end of the grass and weed covered part of the headland a rainwater pond with a little stone dam had perhaps provided drink for cattle, the whole of Fianuis probably being used in summer for the grazing of the cows, while in winter storms made it often inaccessible.

All about the old village, from high up the slope down to the cliff edges, were the cornlands, with the lines of the feannagan or rigs still almost as distinct as they were when sown with barley and oats. More than seventeen acres of arable ground were enclosed with a low stone wall, which followed a winding course from the edge of the rocks at Leac na Sgròb up the slope west of the village, and then turning eastward came down to the cliff at Poll Heallair. From its most northerly point another wall cut over the ridge to the edge of the cliffs above Geodha Blàtha. Immediately north and west of the graveyard a section of feannagan had been separately enclosed at one time by what was probably an older dyke of stones and turf, and the rigs here ran along the slope in the upper portion before turning downhill like almost all the rest in the wider area. Whether or not the arable had been divided according to the number of tenant families living there before 1700 it was impossible to say, but clearly the single shepherd had been able to work as many of the rigs as he wished.

All these features of a vanished life were picked out for Muir and the schoolmaster by the low sun of a fine July evening in 1860. If they looked back down the slope on their way over from Sceapull to Geodha Stoth, they saw the curving lines of the feannagan, the walls, and the low ruins of the village, all with the shadows deepening on their eastward sides, and perhaps too there was still part of a roof on the house of the southwest "inclosure" where the King of Rona had been the last to live. Otherwise there was nothing to catch their attention on the bare island except the little things that would escape the notice of a hurrying visitor; the mooring ring, partly covered with seaweed, the rusting sickle and the abandoned quernstone buried in the long waving grass.

Angus Gunn and the stories of Rona

The books by MacCulloch and Muir must have aroused the interest of many people who, unlike the inhabitants of Ness, had no chance of ever making a visit to Rona. Indeed the next to concern themselves with the island and its history did not go there, but explored Ness instead and "visited" Rona in their imagination by means of the memories and information of others. In particular, they called upon Angus Gunn who was getting on in years but still had a marvellous memory.

The Gunns were yet another Lewis family with origins in Caithness. According to tradition, the first of the name in Lewis came from Wick in order to build a boat for taking supplies to Rona and for bringing sheep back. Who asked him to do the job is not clear, but it could well have been one of the Murrays. He is said to have married a girl in Eoropie.

The first Gunn about whom anything is known was called, according to William Watson, "Iain MacDhomnuill mhic Annuis", John son of Donald son of Angus. He had a half pennyland in Swainbost and kept excellent cattle — Watson told a story of how he sold "one splendid yellow cow" to a drover for fifteen merks. It is just possible that this John was the "John Gun" living at Swainbost in 1792. The only other Gunn family then recorded in Ness was that of Donald in Habost, and most probably John and Donald were related. Later there were Gunns, possibly branches of the old family, in Lionel and Eoropie.

Angus Gunn's father was Donald, who may have been John's eldest son. Born about 1760, he was a crofter fisherman in Habost and later in North Dell, with a house in the old village which lay towards the sea from Baile Griais. In his youth he was caught by the pressgang and went to India as a soldier in the first Seaforth Highlanders, raised in 1778. While in the army he picked up some of the English language which was to prove particularly useful to him on a later occasion. He came back to Dell, married Ann MacFarlane, and had four children among whom Angus was the only son. One daughter, Mary, married in Sandwick, while Margaret married Donald MacLean at number 12 South Dell, and Ann, unmarried, lived with the MacLeans. None of the sisters had children.*

---

* It is also suggested that there was no Mary, but a second son John, who emigrated to Canada with his wife Margaret MacLean.

When Donald left the army he was allowed a pension, which he had to collect at Stornoway once or twice a year. He generally made for the pub on these occasions, and his wife knew well that most of the pension would be drunk away. Thus she decided to accompany him and to join in the drinking. The conversation is said to have gone as follows:

"Well I knew I was a drunkard, but I never knew you were too".
"I thought if I drank as well we would get through the pension quicker".
"Well, it won't last long if the candle is burned at both ends!"

So Donald stopped drinking.

Angus Gunn was born in 1787. Soon after 1800, when he was still a lad, the pressgang came again. They were keen to take Angus with them, but as he was rather young and as his father had suffered the same fate, it was decided after some discussion that he should be left for a year. Donald Gunn with his grasp of English understood this clearly enough, so it was arranged that Angus should go out to Rona where he could not easily be reached and in this way he avoided becoming a soldier.

Fionnlagh Ruadh and his family were in Rona at the time as Daniel Murray told T.S. Muir in 1860. Speaking of the chapel in Rona, Murray described what was left of it "when Angus Gunn was on the island fifty years ago".[179] Since his first daughter was born in 1810 it was probably about 1806 when Angus was there, according to tradition as a youth of 18, but it is not certain how long he stayed. Carmichael, who met him, said that he "lived for many years in the island", but in tradition he is supposed to have been there for only one year.

While on Rona Angus assisted the MacKays to make cheese out of the sheep's milk, catch fish, and kill seals. Returning by one of Alasdair Mac Ruairidh's boats, he lived again in the family home, but it was not long before he married Christina MacKenzie of number 32 South Dell. Eventually they settled in North Dell, first at Baile Griais about 1832. To improve a little on what must have been a meagre living, Angus used to fish along the shore near Airnistean for the farmer, Donald Mac Ailein, and, like many of his neighbours, made whisky in a secret still at Muilinn a' Ghuinnich on the Cross River not far out into the moor. The whisky was sold in Stornoway until a Gress man reported Angus, who was then taken to the town by the "Excise", along with two boys and a sample of their work. The informer received £1 as a reward and the Excise officers destroyed the still, but Angus again seems to have escaped compulsory service.

In 1866 and 1867 when William Watson and Malcolm MacPhail visited him, Angus Gunn was still in North Dell. When Alexander

Carmichael came to see him about 1870, Angus was certainly unable to do outside work:

> "[He] had been an industrious crofter in his day but was now in his eighty-fourth year a bed-ridden cottar. He lived in a miserable house that would have given a stranger to such houses an erroneous impression were he to judge of him by the character of his surroundings."[180]

Carmichael observed that like most cottars or crofters Angus Gunn had received no school education apart from a knowledge of the Gaelic scriptures, yet like them also "he possessed fine natural ability, a great amount of traditional lore, local information and local intelligence, combined with . . . easy well-bred courtesy". It was only possible for the visitor to skim the surface:

> "My limited time and imperfect understanding of the kind courteous old man's impaired enunciation prevented me writing down much of his highly interesting old lore. I did what I could however under the circumstances and noted from his speaking a very curious, a very old and to my thinking a very beautiful hymn. Some curious traditions and graphic stories of the old customs the old people the old saints and the old temples of Ness. It is not easy however to [render] into adequate English the rhythmical runs and graphic alliteration in which the people give these things in Gaelic".[181]

Angus Gunn and Christina MacKenzie had four children. The oldest was Christina, who became known as the Cràg. She is said to have died about 1915 at the age of 105, by which time her years had already given rise to the saying "As old as the Cràg".* She married Alexander Smith from Habost, and her grandfather, Donald, gave them his croft at Lot 14 North Dell. There her husband worked the croft while she spun wool, wove the yarn, and made the material into blankets which she sold for the rent money. There were until recently a few in Ness who could remember Christina, how she kept her faculties until almost the last year of her life and how it was her habit to shade her eyes with her hand. The next child was John, who was born in 1814 and died of pleurisy in 1872. He learned English in the farm house where Donald Mac Ailein employed a tutor for his own children, and he began a smithy and wheelwright business, building a house and forge at Baile Griais. He obtained Lot 8, North Dell, and in 1868 removed to the then Lot 20 where he remained for the rest of his life. Lastly there was Annie, considerably younger than the others, who died at number 11 North Dell about 1900. She married Donald MacDonald, son of Iain Buidhe, and they lived at number 24 North Dell. Donald used to walk over the moor to go fishing from Skigersta.

---

* Alternative information is that she was born in 1812 and was second daughter, Margaret born in 1810 being her older sister.

He was still only a young man when, after an expedition for ling, he became ill with pneumonia and died. Thereafter Annie was deprived of croft number 24 at Whitsunday 1866 in spite of her petition, and so went to care for her father at his house. She left at least three children, Murdo and Christina, neither of whom married, and Mary, who married Norman MacKay grandson of Fionnlagh Ruadh in Skigersta.

The old Lot 20 which had been occupied by John Gunn, son of Angus, and his wife Jane Murray after they left number 8, had a portion of land in Baile Griais which was taken into Dell Farm in 1875. The remainder passed to John's widow as number 19.

Angus Gunn lived for some time after his son John's death in 1872. It is possible that he stayed with Annie, or on croft number 19 which was occupied by his daughter-in-law Jane Gunn and her sons Donald and John, who continued the smith and wheelwright business on the new site, the old smithy having gone with the Baile Griais land to Dell Farm. Perhaps Alexander Carmichael found him here in his miserable dwelling when he came to hear the old man's stories. In a letter of 17th December 1885, Mrs MacLeod in Port of Ness remarked on Carmichael's seeing Angus Gunn, who "could give you accurate information regarding almost anything you wished to know". These words do not mean that Angus was still alive; and indeed he had died at Dell ten years before at the age of 88.

The notes taken by Carmichael on his visit to North Dell are a tantalising record of what Angus Gunn must have said. They are in a private shorthand, and shift to and fro between English and Gaelic without warning. The writing is hasty and at times almost illegible, while in total the several pages can only form a small part of the wealth which was lost at the storyteller's death. In them, nevertheless, lie clues to the ancient folklore of Ness, and especially of Rona.

Angus Gunn had much information about the chapels that stood along the Ness coast from Teampull na Crò Naomh at Galson to Teampull Ronaidh at Eoropie. He told of Niall Odhar who lived at Dùn Othail, and of how the nettles waving in the wind at Babhun Dùn Othail, were growing out of his blood. There were the hidden houses — "taighean falaich" — near the lighthouse at the Butt, and the fairy woman — "gruagach" — who frequented the old Eoropie graveyard, cladh Eoropaidh. The gruagach played a part in the lives of people, and so was respected. Stones with hollows were used as bowls to hold milk for her; there is such a stone on the Habost machair near the boundary with Swainbost, and another in Rona. Angus Gunn told of how a woman out searching for a lamb was taken with her lamb by the "siths" — the fairies — to Rona, and when she returned she described "what the Roney man and his family were doing on a certain Leac na Gruag on top of Si [i.e. Sìthean] in Roney". Each evening they

102

put a mug of milk into three holes and none was left in the morning. In more recent tradition it is said that every evening of his stay Iain Buidhe put milk into the footprint of the woman on "Clach na Gruagaich" and that every morning the hollow was empty.

Carmichael, like William Watson before him, also heard longer stories, of the Vikings, the fairy hills such as Sìthean Balltair on the northern boundary of Dell farm, and the old forts or duns some of which Angus had seen almost entire and shaped like black bottles. The history of the blacksmith Murrays was described, and the remarkable story of Cromanis and the poor woman from Cromarty whom he turned away to his cost. There was too the "long long story how Roney was won and lost", but none caught the attention of the listeners as much as the account of Ronan and his journey to that island in the distant ocean on the back of the "cionaran-crò".

It was unfortunate that Carmichael was not able to spend longer with Angus Gunn, and that he missed talking with Iain Buidhe altogether. Other surviving Rona people would also have had much to tell him. The later generations of the "Buidhe" family in particular were well acquainted with the world of Rona, even those who had never lived there, and it was no wonder that many of them wished to visit the place, and the house, where Iain Buidhe had been year after year long ago. From all these Ness men and women came the familiar stories, and one or two others that Angus Gunn may have known but did not tell Alexander Carmichael, such as the story of Luran.*

One day the cattle of the sea came ashore on Rona. The mermaid followed them and would have taken them back but the people, seeing them ashore, hurriedly took urine between the beasts and the sea and splashed it on the landing place so that they could not return. This had to be done to the cattle as well each morning before letting them out to graze in order to keep them. One day however the herd boy, called Luran, failed to throw the urine over the cattle, and the mermaid, who had been present nearly all the time, returned to the sea's edge. Her voice, or that of the King of the Cattle, called to the animals by their names:

> "Ho! gu'n tig [dith] Sitheag
> Ho! gu'n tig Seothag
> Ho! gu'n tig Crom an taoid [Druim an t-Sobhail]
> Ho! gu'n tig Caoilteag-bhàn [Caoisleach]
> Ho! gu'n tig Donnach mhòr a bhainne bhruich
> > [Donallach mhòr na bainne bhruich]
> > [gu'n tig Gobhal Ard
> > gu'n tig Cuailtean
> > gu'n tig Caircean
> > Thoir mo chrodh a dhachaidh slàn]"

* This story has also been set at Shawbost, Lewis, and elsewhere.

The cattle made for the sea, and the mermaid cried out: "My cattle are here coming, but though the cattle are coming, let the herdsman not come". Luran had been put in charge because he was the most active and the fastest runner in the community, though he fed only on bread and milk. He ran after the cattle and caught the last of them by the tail as it plunged into the sea but he could not keep it. So the cattle went away, and the voice of the mermaid was heard:

"Nach bu luath lòm Luran,
[Mur be cruas arain]
'Nam be lite 'us bainne biadh Lurain
Cha bhiodh laogh nam bò an diugh gun chumail"

How swift and nimble is Luran,
Were it not for the dryness of bread
Had Luran's food been porridge and milk,
No calf or cow would have escaped today".[182]

Iain Buidhe, who must have told this story to his children, is said to have seen the fairy dog — cù sìth — coming after him as he returned from Rona with seven cows belonging to Alasdair Mac Ruairidh.

Iain MacKay was the source of yet another tale about Rona, given by T.S. Muir in his conversational manner. The two men were talking about the shape of the larger chapel extending west from the cell. In the south wall there was the doorway, three and a half feet high, with a small window east of it, and in the eastern gable the entrance to the cell, filled with earth and concealed except for a gap of about eighteen inches at the top. The east gable wall had a bend towards the cell and this was the subject of Iain's story, which aroused Muir's interest because he thought it might explain the odd shape. According to the tradition he heard, the devil was responsible for the bend and not Ronan. The devil found out where Ronan had gone from Ness and followed him to the island to see what he was doing. "It was a wild stormy night — that just before the New Year," said Iain, — "when he landed. I could shew you the place he came to, if we went back to the island again, — not the place any of us would have taken a boat to, but a coarse ugly place, that would tear a boat all to pieces, if there should be anything of a sea on". The devil climbed to the teampull and was about to go in when he looked through the doorway. He saw St. Ronan at the altar, upon which candles burned, and was frightened, so he turned and went down to the point on the shore where he had landed, down below the teampull at a place where the scratches of his claws can still be seen.

"Well?" asked Muir.

"Well — he went down to the sea — the devil did — and raised a tempest a hundred times more terrible than ever, thinking to blow the teampull, and everything in it out of the island; but it was too strong — only, the wall that has the door through it, was driven in so, that Saint Roman, fearing it would burst, had to get up and put his back to it, to keep it and push it even again".

This Ronan did not quite manage to do. Though "the devil kept the wind raging for three nights and three days", Ronan and the sacred candles held the wickedness back, but their strength could not straighten the wall.[183]

With the deaths of Angus Gunn, Iain Buidhe, Iain MacKay, Donald MacLeod and the rest, these stories of Rona faded a little more from the winter firesides of Ness. The fewer people who knew them, the more possible it was to ask questions. How many of the stories had already been forgotten? How old were they? How much of them was history? Yet, in times to come, there would be other, new stories, based on real and sometimes mysterious events, just perhaps as the old stories were. One of the saddest of these events was to happen soon after Alexander Carmichael had visited Ness.

Malcolm MacDonald and Murdo MacKay

In 1883 a different kind of visitor landed on Rona. This was Mr John Swinburne, whose main interest was in birds. His own account describes an adventure in the yacht "Medina" which started in Stornoway on Monday 18th June. He sailed up towards the harbour at Port of Ness where he hoped to find a "pilot", and at 2 a.m. on the Tuesday morning he was woken when they were off the Butt. There was a heavy ground swell beneath a dead calm, and the dinghy was launched with difficulty. Swinburne went ashore:

> "Ness is a very strange place, being a large bay open to the south-east, the top of which is formed by a stretch of beautiful white sand, on which a heavy surf breaks continuously. The sides are formed by broken cliffs, and on the north side of the bay is the so-called harbour, which is merely a slip where the fishermen haul up their boats.
>
> "I had considerable difficulty at first in getting anyone to volunteer to act as pilot, as all the men were just going out to haul their lines, but at last a man of the name of Norman MacLeod came forward. I give the name in case anyone intending to visit Sula Sgeir or Rona should want a good pilot who knows the ground thoroughly. I should strongly advise any future visitor to get a pilot in Ness, as the Stornoway pilots are a terrible set of land-sharks".[184]

Since Swinburne left Ness about 5 a.m. the same morning he must have been looking for a pilot between 2.30 a.m. and 4.30 a.m., not the best of times for finding an unoccupied guide wandering about down at the quay and watching others going out to haul their lines. As it happened, however, he had found Tormod Pìobar, and during the next twelve hours while they sailed northwards he got all the information he could out of his pilot. Norman MacLeod told him how he had lived for some time on Rona looking after the sheep, and that a great many birds nested there, including "a petrel of some sort". About 5 p.m. they sighted both Sula Sgeir and Rona, and towards 7 p.m. they were close in to the former isle and preparing to land. After a brief exploration, during which Norman MacLeod kept careful guard over the gannets, they crossed to Rona where an easy landing was possible. Swinburne hastened to the village because he had been told by his guide that the birds he was looking for, the petrels, were breeding among the ruins. So it happened that the first naturalist followed the surveyor in damaging the ancient walls. "We were all soon at work", Swinburne wrote,

> "hauling out large stones, and scraping with our hands, guided by the strong musky odour which pervaded the inhabited burrows which run through and through the thick walls of the old buildings, the latter of which, mixed with earth and turf as they were, afforded unequalled facilities to the birds for the purpose".[185]

Within five minutes "the first petrel with its egg was brought to light", and soon the searchers had dug out twenty two more, undoubtedly upsetting more walls in the course of their effort. Then, still in a hurry, Swinburne and his companions sailed away, their visit leaving now a strange impression of not much more than hasty plunder, as if they had been pirates like those feared by the Rona people of old.

Swinburne was not very concerned about the ruins, the descriptions by MacCulloch and Muir being quite sufficient for him. He did notice the thickness of the house walls and the sunken floors, and made a few other notes, but these were no more than random scraps of information. He remarked that Rona had been uninhabited since Donald MacLeod's return to Lewis "except for a few days at the annual sheep-shearing at the end of July", although this was inconsistent with his statement that Tormod Pìobair had lived there for some time. He noticed only forty or fifty sheep, and these were very wild, whereas in former times the Murrays had kept up to two hundred. There were "occasional losses from their falling over rocks or being stolen by the crews of passing vessels", and Swinburne heard that on one occasion shipowners sent money in payment for a stolen sheep. It is a pity that he and others like him did not follow up the story of Rona more closely, and write fuller accounts of the management of the island in their own time.

106

As it happened, the year of Swinburne's visit, 1883, was the one that saw a break in the old Murray tenancy, and the beginning of the MacKenzies' unhappy lease. Apart from the yacht party, and the annual clipping, there was probably no other interruption to the lonely peace of the abandoned island until the summer of 1884, when, in the third week of June, Malcolm MacDonald and Murdo MacKay went to stay there.[186]

Malcolm MacDonald, Calum Mhic Mhurchaidh Cuthail, was born in 1818 and was in Rona as a lad, making cheese and doing other general work. He probably lived with one of the last shepherd families, although it is said that he was there with Alan Campbell, who was one of the three young men on the island in 1841. When he came back from Rona Malcolm became a crofter and boatbuilder in Eorodale, but he went out to the island again for what turned out to be an unrewarding fishing season. In 1876 he led the party of Ness men who crossed to the Sutherland coast where one of them, Dòmhnull Seònaid, climbed onto the stack of Handa for birds. There is much less known about Murdo MacKay, called Murchadh Bhragair, a younger man who was a crofter and weaver in Lionel. It is certain that they were bold and intelligent men, who were frequently asked for advice by their neighbours, and who both played a prominent part in the life of the Free Church in Ness. Surprisingly, therefore, a dispute with their minister caused them to go to Rona. It was said by some that the Reverend MacBeth had baptised the daughter of the schoolmaster at home but had refused to baptise another man's child although the mother was too ill to go to church; others thought that a layman had been improperly appointed as preacher. Three men raised objections, Malcolm MacDonald, Murdo MacKay, and one known as the catechist, An Ceisdear. It is supposed that there was a prophecy which stated that not one of the three should have a natural death, and indeed the catechist went missing, neither he nor his body ever being found. The other two left for Rona and an almost equally mysterious fate.

The circumstances of their going were described by a visitor in an account written on 7th December 1885:

"In fine weather, and only then, it is possible to land on the Island with comparative safety. There being no beach it is a matter of difficulty even in fine weather to effect a landing from a small boat. Sometimes the Island is visited by the crews of passing ships and on these occasions there is usually a diminution observed in the number of the sheep. Probably the hardy mariners have a weakness for good fresh mutton — and the Rona sheep make proverbially good mutton — or at all events they consider it desirable to remove a few as mementoes of their visit! . . .

"The Farmer Tenants (two) have had numerous applications for the office of shepherd on Rona and among others . . . Malcolm MacDonald and Murdo MacKay have been applicants for that office. Last year they were chosen, and on 20th June 1884 were landed and left on the Island with a plentiful supply of provisions".

Malcolm MacDonald's son, Donald, a boy of fourteen who was working in a shop in Stornoway, went out in the boat with the two men and slept between them on their first night in Rona.

There was some apprehension at the departure of the two men from Ness. A daughter of one of them is said to have twice removed her father's clothes from the chest to prevent him from going and the bodies of sheep were ominously washed up on the Ness shore. Nevertheless they did go, supposedly to erect fences to keep the sheep from going over the rocks, and they made themselves reasonably comfortable by rebuilding the central room of the old "inclosure" against the southwest wall of the graveyard. They constructed from the ruin a single-roomed house, with a chimney in the north gable wall and in the other a doorway sheltered by a porch. They are supposed to have also used stones from the other "inclosures", especially Iain Buidhe's house. According to the 1885 account,

"After being left on the Island on 20th June 1884 the shepherds were again visited by friends from Lewis on 13th August following when they were found to be in good health and spirits and they declared that they had no desire to leave Rona till the following Spring. They then informed their friends that four days previously they had had a visit one misty morning from some men from a passing ship who, in spite of all the remonstrances of the shepherds, cooly removed four sheep. There was a name on the stern of their boat, but the shepherds being unable to read it the perpetrators of the outrage could not be traced.*

"On 23rd August thereafter some people from Lewis again visited Rona and found everything as before. They saw that the shepherds were well supplied with provisions and that they were in good health and spirits. After the departure of these visitors the Island does not seem to have been visited till 22nd April 1885".[187]

So the darkness and damp chill of winter closed round the two men. In October an expedition to the island was organised in Ness but was prevented by stormy weather. Another attempt was made in November but again storms made the journey impossible. The men were on the island under familiar conditions. They had to milk the sheep, make cheese, kill seals and render blubber to oil. Anything above the rent quota of the produce was theirs. So apart from their shepherding, the men occupied themselves in killing seals, which they did with stout sticks. They rendered oil from the blubber and stored the

* It is probably this episode that is recorded in a Ness story of how an old Hull fisherman confessed that when he was a young cook on board a fishing boat he visited an island in the north of Scotland and helped to ruin two old men.

sealskins. After New Year and the end of the seals' breeding season, they cannot have had much to do.

The spring came and the weather improved, and it was time for a visit to the island. On 22nd April 1885 the "Lilly", a hired smack, left with a party of Nessmen who were taking out some sheep and provisions for the shepherds. An account written a few months later tells what then happened:

> "On landing the party were surprised that the shepherds did not approach to welcome them and on proceeding towards the hut and observing that no smoke issued from the chimney their apprehensions that something was wrong increased.
>
> "Arrived at the hut a ghastly sight met their view. Lying on the ground outside — near the door — was the dead body of Malcolm Macdonald; and inside stretched on the floor and dressed as if for burial, the dead body of his companion Murdo MacKay".

When reported in Ness, the discovery shocked the people. Several versions of how the men were found spread through the community, and before long there were reports that in some houses there had been fore-warnings of a disaster in Rona. Mrs Gunn understood from a verse of Jeremiah that something was wrong. Alexander Carmichael, hearing a rumour of prophetic dreams, wrote to Mrs MacLeod of Ocean Villa, who spoke to a woman from South Dell in Barvas, "Fionnaghal Bheag", and took down her words:

> "My name is Flora Gillies, or Macdonald. I am 68 years of age. I am a widow for the last 14 years. My husband's name was Colin Macdonald. Murdo MacKay who died in Rona was a cousin of my husband's. Neither Murdo MacKay nor Malcolm Macdonald were related to myself. I did *not* dream a dream *before* the smack 'Lily' went to Rona and found the two men dead there; but I had a strong presentiment that something was wrong at Rona owing to certain texts of Scripture which kept continually before my mind in connection with Murdo MacKay and Malcolm Macdonald and so strong was the feeling, that I went down to Ness to try and persuade MacKay and Macdonald's friends to get the Lessee of the Island of Rona to send a Boat to help the men . . . I do not think the smack 'Lily' was sent any sooner to Rona on account of my talk with the friends. *After* the smack returned and I heard of the deaths, I dreamed that Murdo MacKay stood before me and repeated the first two verses of the 73rd psalm . . . and then vanished. I saw no more of them since".

In the village of Habost, it is said, there was a family which was in touch with ghosts or spirits. One evening, after supper, the young son made to go outside, but his father called out: "Have you got anything important to do? Can you wait an hour?" "Yes, alright", was the reply. "I am expecting a knock in an hour's time — it came last night. Go to the door when it comes, but don't approach him". The knock came. The son opened the door and took a step forward, whereupon the visitor retreated a step and then vanished. "Did you recognise him?" asked the father. "No, unless he was one of the men in Rona". "There's somethng wrong in Rona". So the boat went out and found the men dead.

Accounts agree that Murdo MacKay was found in the house, prepared for burial, and that his companion Malcolm MacDonald was found outside the door. Some say that Malcolm had put sacking around his friend and had made a trolley with wheels to take him to the graveyard. Malcolm's son Donald said that Murdo MacKay was found dead lying on the turf seat in the house and that he was covered with a plaid. Mrs MacLeod discovered one or two other details:

> "One of the men who was in the 'Lily', who helped to bury the bodies, tells me, that Murdo MacKay died first. Murdo was found inside of the house lying with his head towards the fire-place and his feet towards the door. His head was covered with a woollen shirt and his highland plaid was neatly tucked in round him, showing that Malcolm's hands had performed the last sad task to his companion".

According to his son, Malcolm MacDonald had been on his way to the well with a pail and a pan when he collapsed just outside the house. He was found "lying as if he had just fallen asleep". Mrs MacLeod heard that Malcolm, who was a strong stalwart man, was supposed to have been ill and weak before Murdo died, otherwise he would have made a coffin for his friend and buried him. It was strange that Malcolm MacDonald's body was found next to an improvised fireplace in the porch, and a possible explanation seemed to be that Malcolm, unable to lift the dead Murdo, had been compelled to move outside where within a short time he had been overcome by his own illness, exhaustion and exposure.

Those from the smack "Lilly" who made the dreadful discovery hastily rolled the bodies in canvas and buried them together in the Rona graveyard. After their return to Ness, the news spread far and wide, and within a few days the Daily Mail reported events. The paper was not quite accurate, getting dates wrong and switching the names of the men, and of course it gave space to the prophetic dreams of "a woman in Barvas". Whether or not as a result of the article, the matter was brought up in Parliament, and because it was felt that the men might not have died naturally "the Crown authorities" ordered the Stornoway procurator fiscal to investigate. On 30th May 1885 the Oban Times reported that he "has been waiting on an opportunity to proceed with the medical men to the island, but he was specially desired not to incur the expense of chartering a steamer". The captain of the cutter "Vigilant", a MacDonald, agreed to land the party in

Rona in the course of his fishery protection duties, and so on Tuesday 26th May at 8 a.m. the deputy procurator fiscal John Ross, Dr Roderick Ross of Borve and Dr Finlay MacKenzie of Stornoway, Police Superintendant Gordon and John Weir of Swainbost — "one of those who found the bodies and interred them" — all landed at Stoth to exhume the dead. With them was Donald MacDonald, Malcolm's son. He had been annoyed at the crew of the "Lilly" for not bringing home the bodies and had now gone out "at his urgent request", taking two coffins.

In the graveyard "a long post-mortem examination was made by the two medical gentlemen". There was no sign of injury, and it appeared that the two men had fed sufficiently well for their bodies to have been "in good condition". In Malcolm MacDonald's stomach were found a few grains of undigested oatmeal, "and in MacKay's a little brown fluid". It was concluded that the latter had died of acute inflammation of the right lung and left kidney, while MacDonald had indeed been overcome by cold, exposure and exhaustion. Donald MacDonald made things out a little differently:

"My father died of heart failure and Murdo MacKay of kidney trouble caused by a kick he got from a horse as a boy".

When the examination was finished, the remains were put in the coffins and buried again.

Afterwards a search was made at the house. A pot had been on the makeshift fire outside, and within was plenty of food. A few possessions were packed up and taken to the boat, among them an object which attracted much interest. It was a board of pitch pine, described by the Oban Times as a stick, and in another account as "a bar of red pine wood, evenly and accurately dressed, 2 feet long and 1⅛ inch in the side". Donald MacDonald said it was one foot square. The two men had made this a calendar, by cutting notches round the edge, a small one for a week-day and a larger, deeper one for Sunday, and for the end of the month a cut right across. Assuming that the first notch was cut on 20th June 1884, it was calculated that the last one represented Tuesday 17th February 1885, at about which time it was thought the men must have died. The last notches were less well made as if the maker was growing weak. Through a hole in the calendar a looped cord had been threaded, by which to hang it up. Donald MacDonald claimed such of his father's belongings as remained, but some public authority claimed the calendar and it was placed in the old Stornoway Town Hall, where it was destroyed by the fire which burnt the Hall in 1918. "If they had left the board with me", said Donald MacDonald, "I would have it to this day".

Four implements which Norman MacKenzie, one of the two

tenants, had given to Malcolm MacDonald were also returned. These were a blacksmith-made hammer all in one piece, an adze, a saw and an axe. They were brought back to Norman and put to use at home. Eventually the hammer was lost and the adze, which had served on the croft as a croman or hand hoe for lifting potatoes, wore out. Norman's son and a friend, two small boys, were playing one day with the saw when an uncle arrived "with a bright, shining saw from Sheffield". The uncle showed the boys an impressive trick. He bent his saw so that the point of the blade could be slipped through the hole in the handle. But when the boys tried this later with their own old saw, Malcolm's saw from Rona, the long blade snapped and the implement was of no more use. Only the axe blade, mounted on a replacement shaft, survives as a reminder of those valuable articles once taken out to the island in the ocean.

The "Vigilant" made a slow return from Rona. After being becalmed several times she at last reached port on the morning of Friday 29th May, and the affair of the two unfortunate men seemed over. Not long afterwards, however, another boat visited the island and added one further part to the story.

At the time the post-mortem expedition was being planned, in mid May 1885, a fishing smack called the "George and Mary" sailed from its home port of Grimsby and made north on what, according to a member of the crew, "we call a 'Country Voyage' ".[188] The intention was "to fish in Scotland off Cape Wrath". The crew consisted of John Wadmore, skipper, James Pringle, mate, William Campbell, George Blendell, Robert MacCulloch, George Miller and George Clarkson, known as "Curly George". The owners of the smack were the skipper and his half brother, Henry Smithers, a fish salesman in Grimsby, and the members of the crew were mostly young men in their twenties recruited on the basis of sharing the expenses and the profits. Only Robert MacCulloch had been on previous voyages with the same smack.

At first things went smoothly. The men on board were relaxed and the black mongrel dog which had been taken along lay on the deck in the sun. Then, on what was perhaps the last stretch of the journey up the east coast before turning west through the Pentland Firth, rougher weather must have closed in and the main sail was lost. The "George and Mary" put in to Stromness in Orkney to await the arrival of a new sail. After a period which the different members of the crew described as being anything between eight and fourteen days the sail had still not arrived, so the skipper became impatient and decided to leave without it. They moved west and started to fish for cod off Whiten Head and Cape Wrath. In continued bad weather the catches were poor and after five or six weeks spent rather fruitlessly they moved over to Rona for the last few days before returning home. Here luck was no better, and, in spite of provisioning by the skipper himself before leaving Grimsby, supplies began to run low. George Miller said that "At the time we reached Rona we had no eatables on board the smack except fish and biscuits"; William Campbell thought that their only food at this stage was "biscuits and potatoes"; but the cook said they had potatoes, flour, a little bit of ham, a little sugar, and "plenty of fish, both live and salt".

So the Grimsby men rocked uncomfortably off Rona with no fishing success and little to eat apart from the fish they had caught. On the morning of June 26th the skipper decided to take four of the crew ashore on Rona to look for water, and at about 11.30 a.m. or noon the landing party, Wadmore, Pringle, Campbell, Blendell and Miller, lowered the dinghy into the water, put five 9 gallon water-casks into it, and made for a landing on the island. They got ashore safely and began to explore. Later James Pringle declared that although "We had on board the Smack a black dog which was a cross between a Retriever and a shepherd", and which might have been useful in any attempt to catch sheep, "We did not take the Bitch on shore with us". They soon found that Rona was uninhabited.

None of these men had been to Rona before. They knew nothing about it. It must therefore have been with some surprise that they came across the "Hut or Bothy . . . sometime occupied and possessed by Malcolm MacDonald and Murdo MacKay sometime Shepherds on the said Island of Rona, now deceased". The "hut" was still furnished with supplies and equipment left there not out of carelessness but in accordance with traditional understanding of the significance of property. Pringle told how "We entered a hut which we saw in the island and we took from the hut various articles which we saw there". Campbell said that the articles taken included a small cask of butter, about three pounds of brown sugar and two pounds of tea, but later the amount of tea was put at about three pounds and the sugar at about a stone. In addition a box containing about six pounds of soft soap was taken, along with two dinner plates, a basin, a grindstone and a "tin filler". No-one said he had even seen, far less removed, tongs and an iron "crook", but, according to the mate Pringle, "We also saw lying outside the hut a piece of canvas, about two yards long, of which the skipper took possession".

Naturally there were differing opinions on who did what, but the crew generally said they had followed the instructions of the skipper. After leaving the hut the visitors put the small articles into the boat. "As to the Grindstone, while it was rolled down at Rona it got broken and I do not recollect whether it was taken on board or not". Then it was the turn of the sheep which, seemingly uncared for, ranged over

The crew of the 'Alert' pose for a photograph. The 'Alert' was a steam drifter from Banff, one of several fishing in the Minch in 1936.
(photo. Robert Atkinson)

114

the grass and rocks. "We also saw a good many sheep on the island", said the mate. "We caught two of the sheep, a big one and a little one. The big one was a Ewe and the little one was a lamb. The Skipper killed the big one on the island, and we put the carcase and also the lamb into the boat along with the other articles". He added that George Miller, one of the shore party, killed the lamb almost as soon as it was put aboard the smack. Then he changed his mind and said that Miller had killed it when still on Rona. Miller himself, however, made out that they had caught two very small sheep, that the skipper had killed one of them and that he couldn't remember who had killed the other one. Campbell said that two small and one large sheep had been caught, that the two small had been killed on the island and the large one on the smack. The cook, "Curly George", who had stayed on board the smack all this time with MacCulloch, stated that when the dinghy returned, about 3 p.m., "They brought with them some wild birds and three sheep — two small ones and a large one", as well as the domestic articles, and "I think all of the sheep had been killed". He saw no sign of canvas, tongs, iron crook or tin filler, and Miller thought he had seen the canvas left lying near the shore.

"Curly George" told what happened next. "After bringing the sheep and the other articles which they had brought along with them along with the sheep they had dinner on board the smack and then proceeded to the island a second time". The reason for this return visit was made clear in the course of the meal, when the cook heard the others say "something about some casks of oil they had seen on the island". Again the skipper was held responsible. James Pringle said that Wadmore had told the rest of his party that he had seen a number of casks with livers in them. "He said we might as well take them as anybody else, as they did not belong to anybody". So they went back for these casks, the skipper taking cork "which he said was to bung the casks with". When they landed again, apparently at Geodha Stoth, the skipper led them to where the casks were, six of them "lying at one spot near our landing place", another one a bit away from the rest near the shore. "We first went for the single Cask, rowing along to a spot near to it. We put a bung into the Cask, then put the Cask into the Water and towed it after the boat. We then returned with the boat to our original landing place, and after putting bungs in the four or five casks that lay together, we rolled them down to the shore, put them into the water and towed them out to the Smack". Meanwhile, on board the smack, the sheep had been skinned and the skins thrown over the side.

Collecting the casks had taken nearly three hours. "Curly George" Clarkson saw the party return, "towing astern of the small boat a number of casks, I think six. These Casks were put on board the

Smack. The Casks had oil and blubber in them, but what kind I do not know. The Casks were all put below. I did not hear any one say anything about them". Apparently there had been seven casks on Rona, six of them in a group, the other separate, but only six had been taken because, while they were about three quarters full, the seventh had very little in it. The water-casks brought on the smack from Grimsby were left on the grass of the island.

In addition to the water-casks the smack held three more which were described as "Liver-casks", branded with a "B" mark at one end and "the ordinary size, namely thirty six Gallon Casks". When the smack reached Rona two of them held cod liver and the third was empty. The Rona casks were the same size though not marked, and appeared to have been used for paraffin at one time. Though the skipper declared "the stuff in the casks was whale oil", they in fact contained the oil and blubber of seals which had been killed and processed by MacDonald and MacKay. Some sorting out of all these containers was necessary, and once they were together on the smack this was quickly done. The oil was strained "from the livers in the liver casks and . . . from the blubber in the Rona casks"; it was then all mixed together and put back into some, if not all, of the Rona casks. Without having achieved their original purpose in visiting the island because they could not find the springs, the crew then thought of leaving for home.

The next morning there was not a breath of wind. "We lay becalmed for a day or two", Clarkson remembered, "and then proceeded to Loch erribol for water. This would be about three days after the articles I have mentioned were brought from Rona. On leaving Loch erribol, we put in at Tolma where we put ashore two bags of salt and got in exchange some tobacco. The Skipper also got a letter there. That same day we left for Stromness where we arrived next morning". At some point probably on the voyage from Rona to Loch Eriboll in Sutherland an attempt was made to eat the sheep. According to the cook "All the three sheep were in poor condition", but "we were able to eat and did eat the flesh". The rest might not have agreed with the last part of this statement. James Pringle said that "We cooked a part of the Ewe and also of the Lamb, but both of them looked so thin and bad that I could not look at them, and I came out of the Cabin where the food was spread and left the others of the crew there". The sheep carcases were thrown overboard before the smack reached Stromness.

The visit to the old Orkney "capital" proved more worthwhile than the previous one. The mainsail had arrived and was collected. The fishermen then set off southwards. They called in at Fraserburgh, Peterhead and Aberdeen. "The five who had gone ashore at Rona

116

went ashore at Peterhead. This was to try to get the oil sold as I understood. The oil was not sold there. The five who had gone ashore told me that they were offered one shilling and two pence a gallon for it. The same five hands went ashore at Aberdeen. When they came back they led me to understand they had an offer for the oil, but I do not know what it was". George Miller remembered only the visit to Aberdeen where the skipper went alone into the town — "He took a sample of the rich oil with him in a bottle". It seems that no sales were made anywhere and that the casks remained on board. In the course of the return journey to Grimsby "the Crew used the whole of the sugar, the tea and the butter brought from Rona. We also used part of the soap". At least two and perhaps four of the six Rona casks were thrown overboard. "They were empty at that time".

George Clarkson described their arrival at Grimsby. "On our reaching Grimsby we put ashore part of the fish on to the Pontoon. I forget whether this was the day of our arrival or the following day. The day after we had put ashore some of the fish, we put on the Pontoon the rest of the fish we had on board. We lay in the Roads at the time we put ashore the first lot of fish. On the occasion of our putting ashore the second lot, the Vessel was lying at the Pontoon. On the same day that we put on shore the second lot of fish we also put on shore the casks containing the oil". The mate said that there were four or five casks of oil, probably including the two B-marked barrels into which the skipper himself had put part of the strained oil at the beginning of the homeward voyage. Miller said there were three casks of fish liver, two full and one half full, which were also disposed of at Grimsby. Mr Smithers received the fish, while the skipper John Wadmore went off with the casks; Clarkson vaguely remembered the skipper saying that the oil fetched £8. All that remained to do was distributing the proceeds among the crew. They had been away nine weeks.

In their accounts of what happened at the end of the voyage the members of the crew seemed unable to say exactly what they made out of it. "The same day that we put the casks ashore the Skipper gave the mate a Sovereign (£1) and gave each of the rest of us half a sovereign". So said George Clarkson, whose version of events went on: "Next day we met on the Smack for a settlement. The Skipper told us we were each two shillings and two pence in debt and so we did not get anything. There was a written paper produced by the Skipper. Those of the hands that could read looked at the Bills which the Skipper produced. What we were entitled to have received was a share of the money that the fish and the oil had fetched after deducting our share of the Provisions. I did not understand anything about what the Skipper was to do with the Rona oil. I suppose we were all entitled to a share of the Rona oil as well as to a share of the oil from the livers of the

Cod we had caught. I now recollect that George Miller did not receive any money at all". From this it is difficult to tell what exactly Clarkson did get by way of pay and clearly he was reluctant to admit to any connection with the Rona oil. Pringle said the crew received no share of the proceeds from any of the oil, but that the skipper gave each man half a crown, and this was confirmed by Miller. Whether the sum bore any relationship to what was in the bill which the skipper produced Pringle himself did not know because "I am no scholar and don't know what was in it", but he himself was paid two shillings a week for acting as mate. It is probable that Clarkson meant half a crown rather than half a sovereign, that each crew member was given half a crown for his nine weeks away, and that some who were in debt received hardly anything at all.

Successful police work meant that by the beginning of November 1885 skipper Wadmore, Campbell, Miller, Pringle and "Curly George" Clarkson were in prison in Stornoway awaiting trial. The declarations made by the four crew members, taken on 5th and 19th November, contain the recollections of these individuals, and, in spite of the occasional official phrasing such as "proceeded to Loch erribol", a feeling of personal, first-hand experience survives. There is variation in detail as is only to be expected, and a sense of uneasiness about taking stuff from the island which might have been expressed at the time or might have been born in the Stornoway jail. The oil caused particular concern. The mate James Pringle claimed that before making the second trip to the island for it he and Robert MacCulloch tried to stop the skipper from going; "indeed I was swearing about it", said Pringle, but the skipper had said "Come on, it is as well that we should have it as anybody else". It was the skipper, the others said, who "took entire charge", who told them to take the articles from the "hut", and who suggested the removal of sheep and oil, but Pringle admitted that no one had tried to dissuade him from taking the sheep. Clarkson, who had remained on board the smack, put himself at a distance from the actual taking of the goods. "I did not hear any of them say that it was wrong to take the oil and other articles from an uninhabited island. I should think they knew it was wrong without anybody saying it". William Campbell was perhaps rather more open in his remarks: "Anybody would have taken the things as we did. It was a very tempting thing to take them from an uninhabited island". They had, he said, talked about the oil after it was aboard the smack. "We saw it might get us into trouble, and we said among ourselves that it would be best to put it ashore again, but it began to blow fresh and so we could not get to the island, we therefore sailed off".

118

Clarkson also heard this conversation and told of how breeze and fog had made another landing impossible; but he also remarked on the dead calm which overtook them next morning and prevented them for "a day or two" from sailing to Loch Eriboll. The issue of the articles taken from Rona still continued to trouble them after they left the Sutherland coast, according to the mate: "On our way home to Grimsby Robert MacCulloch and I sometimes spoke about what we had done. We said what a pity it was that we had taken the things as they were of no use to us. We did not think there was anything wrong in taking the Sheep as they did not seem to belong to anybody". In fact the items of food had been of use for they had all been consumed on the return journey. The grindstone had been broken and abandoned on the island, and the tin filler had been forgotten, but the plates and basin were still on board the smack at the time of the trial. As for the oil, it proved of some value to the skipper at least. Clarkson said that "The Skipper never told me or any of the others, so far as I heard, what account we were to give of the oil if any enquiries should be made about it"; but Pringle remembered that on the way home the skipper had told the others that if they were asked about the oil they were to say "we had picked it up".

There was no question that the skipper and crew of the "George and Mary" had removed the several articles from Rona. All that the court had really to consider was whether there was any excuse and how seriously to take the mate's observations that the sheep and other items "did not seem to belong to anybody", and the skipper's remark, "I don't see any signboards or anything here". Miller admitted that they knew they were doing wrong but did not like to go against the skipper's orders, and the court had also to determine how far the skipper had to take responsibility for what was seen as a theft. After all the men in prison were accused of "wickedly and feloniously" stealing the items all described as belonging still to "Finlay MacKenzie Farmer and Shopkeeper" and "Norman MacKenzie, Farmer and Fisherman", both of Habost and "joint Tenants or occupants of the said Island". There was a "jury" or "assize" of forty-five men, mostly shopkeepers and tradesmen of Stornoway, and there were ten witnesses. Among the latter were some familiar figures: John Ross Sheriff Clerk Depute, James Gordon Superintendant of Police, Hector Smith Sergeant of Police, Finlay MacKenzie, Norman MacKenzie, John Weir "sometime Shopkeeper and now residing at Swainibost", Donald MacDonald labourer residing at Eorodale, William Fanthorp 16 Yarborough Street, Grimsby, Robert MacCulloch fisherman, Freshney Street, Grimbsy, and George Blendell fisherman 5 Central

Vale, Nelson Street, Grimsby. The decision was reached in early January 1886; the crew members were sentenced to two months imprisonment, the skipper to eight months.*

Yachtsmen and Naturalists

By chance the raiders only just escaped being caught in the act by another naturalist who happened to reach Rona a few days before them on 16th June 1885.[189] Since 1870, "when he first visited these Western Isles of Scotland on a collecting trip", J.A. Harvie-Brown had regularly returned to record and often to shoot the animals and birds which were so abundant in the area. He and a friend, H.G. Barclay of Norwich, sailed in a hired or borrowed yacht from Stornoway to Ness on 10th June 1885, much as Swinburne had done two years before, and similarly they looked for a guide. They found the same one, as Harvie-Brown recorded in his journal:

> "Sent boat ashore for pilot and *Norman* MacLeod (of Rona fame) came aboard, and agreed for £2 a week to take us back to Gress — as we could not safely lie at Ness — lie there till our start — safe from all winds — and go to Rona and Soulisgeir . . . Glass rising".

From Norman MacLeod the naturalists picked up odd bits of information which were duly noted; "There are about 100 sheep on Rona, the rent of which latter is about £30 paid by N. McL."

It is not made clear whether Norman MacLeod was a subtenant to Finlay and Norman MacKenzie at this time, and other reports suggest there were about 200 sheep on the island. "Plenty of good water on Rona according to N. McL (which until I see it!??)". And of course there was the recent unhappy discovery:

> "The two men who died there lately died from special diseases and not *want* as they had plenty of mutton, meal and water(?) One died of heart complaint and the other of some chest disease".

Perhaps the information was not quite accurate, but the visitors were clearly more concerned about the chances of landing than anything else:

* The "assize" included "Donald MacFarquhar cartwright Bayhead Stornoway" and Murdo MacFarquhar farmer, North Dell, Ness. On 4th January 1886 Murdo MacFarquhar sent a note to Mr John Ross to excuse himself from attendance at the jury because he was in poor health. He enclosed a medical certificate from Dr Roderick Ross which stated that he was "at present suffering from an attack of Catarrhal Bronchitis (a complaint to which he is subject in the cold season)" and should not make the journey from "Mill House" at North Dell to Stornoway. A day later, 5th January 1886, Dr Ross sent a similar note stating that Finlay MacKenzie could not appear as a witness because he was confined to bed.

120

"The difficulties of landing are greatly exaggerated according to N. McL (before he was engaged by us). He said we can land in *any wind* if moderate and not too much swell on. Believe not without visual proof".

So they went south to Gress. During the night the wind turned southeast and after 2 a.m. blew hard over Broad Bay. They thought it best to run for Stornoway, "and a fine lively kick up we had of it, the 'You Nasty' as we have rechristened the old tub of a thing instead of *Eunice* — taking blue water in over her stern quarter in a disgraceful manner and leaking at every pore". Harvie-Brown did not think the yacht was fit to go to Rona, and what made it worse, it belonged to a Glasgow or Greenock owner, "a somewhat illiterate man". They reached Stornoway at 6.30 in the morning of 11th June, and Harvie-Brown wrote in his journal:

"I was drowned out of my cabin about 5 a.m. Lay all day. Ugh!!"

At 8 a.m. on 12th June "two native gents came aboard", requesting a member of the party to open a bazaar in Stornoway for the Free Kirk, and so Harvie-Brown "Lay all day again". Then at 3.30 a.m. on the 13th, with the light strengthening, they set off for Rona:

"When we passed the Butt of Lewis, steering straight for Rona, it was found that a heavy ground swell was still coming in off the N.W. but there was little wind. Norman — the pilot — however is doubtful of our being able to anchor off Rona if the swell continues, or of landing on Rona. The day is lovely, but oh that nasty swell!! It is very tantalizing".

At 8 o'clock they decided to give up the attempt, and changing course they made for Lochinver on the mainland, reaching port about 2 p.m. and remaining there until the following morning. Then they tried again. With dawn they left the shelter of Lochinver harbour and went north past Handa, but "bad luck attends us", and such a heavy swell caught them that they had to take refuge in Loch Laxford. A day passed and their luck changed. The morning of 16th June was quiet and peaceful, full of promise.

The "Eunice" left Loch Laxford at 10 a.m., in a calm sea with only a ground swell and "no long rollers". There was no wind, and the horizon was clear though a slight heat haze lay over land and water. The weather looked settled fine. At 1.15 p.m. they sighted Rona, and three hours later, after having had time to make a sketch of the island as seen from the southeast, they came in and "Landed with great ease . . . round the point where the birds are seen flying in the sketch, on the East side, a fine sheltered bay, where the Yacht let go her anchor".

The landing party, which included "The Steward Cameron, Oban; Norman McLeod, and Angus", as well as Harvie-Brown and Barclay, drew up the dinghy onto the rocks and made directly for the village area. They had with them two boxes of biscuits, two of sardines, one bottle and two flasks of whisky, and "Not trusting the accounts of 'Spring' water we heard [we] took one of Silvers felted bottles with water". They were also armed with a circular bandage, a parcel of lint, another of oiled silk, two boxes of "Bryant and May", a "Box Vesuvians to save the matches", binoculars, a cake of soap, string, a substance called "Tamar India" and two empty boxes, one for any eggs they found and one "Small Box for Petrels Eggs". Harvie-Brown, intent upon heaving up stones from the village ruins to uncover the petrels, had wanted to bring heavier equipment as well:

> "we would have taken a crow-bar but Norman said there were two spades on shore. Sequel showed that the crow-bar would have been a great assistance and saved time — the spades were at the houses, where the two poor fellows died this spring, and which are still in habitable condition".

When they reached "the Fork Tailed Petrels breeding place amongst the ruins of the old village", they set to work, heaving out the stones from the walls and digging away the earth so as to uncover the birds in their burrows. After an hour and a half they had discovered several forktailed and two stormy petrels. Some of the former Harvie-Brown released in the air so as to watch their flight, and "I would like to have tossed up the Stormy Petrels too in order to compare the flight of the two species, but greed, and the fact that they had not previously been recorded as inhabiting Rona prevailed". They also found many forktailed petrel nests:

> "The single egg of each bird lay at the end of the tunnellings deep amongst the stones and sea-pink covered turf-walls of the long since deserted village. Our men worked heartily with spades and arms, but we took all the eggs ourselves except four, I think of Barclays — he got in all 15 and I took 9 but had one broken by Angus foot".

Harvie-Brown remarked on the ruins, the luxuriant grass growing over nearly a foot of good soil in the rigs, and the place "some little distance from the houses" where the turf had been cut for fuel. His interest in the scattered piles of loose stones was chiefly aroused by the fact that wheatears had nested in them. As the evening was coming on, there was little time to take any closer look at the settlement, but the visitors did go into the recently abandoned house, where they saw the grinding stone, tea, sugar, butter, soap and other provisions which the Grimsby fishermen were shortly to plunder. Then they left the village, and crossing the ridge descended Leathad Fhianuis in a hurry:

> "The dirt and heat and petrel oil which the birds freely squirted over us, made us extremely glad to have a long pull at Silvers water bottle".

122

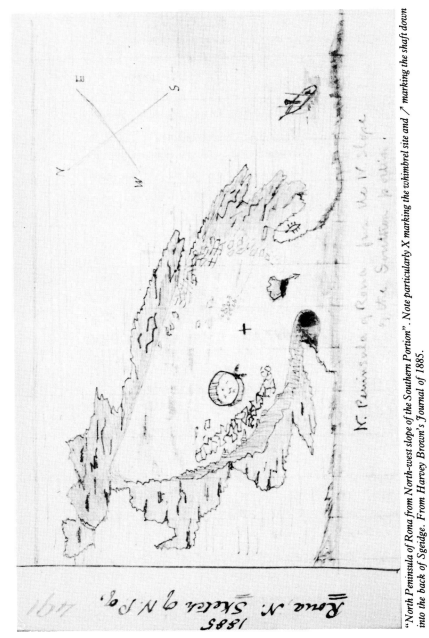

"North Peninsula of Roma from North-west slope of the Southern Portion". Note particularly X marking the whimbrel site and ⌐ marking the shaft down into the back of Sgeidge. From Harvey Brown's Journal of 1885.

Sketch of the cave at Sgeildige by J.A. Harvie Brown from Harvey Brown & T.E. Buckley. 'A Vertebrate Fauna of the Outer Hebrides' Edinburgh 1888 p. liv.

As they went down the slope Harvie-Brown paused to make a quick sketch of Fianuis. They had said that they would be aboard again at 6 o'clock, and there were only a few minutes to go, but this did not prevent the two naturalists at least making a dash along the headland. The steam whistle sounded before they had gone very far, but they saw two whimbrels "evidently breeding", and Harvie-Brown marked the spot on his sketch with a X. There was no time to look for the nest of these unusual birds.

> "Had it rested with me alone I would have heeded that whistle very little, just as on previous occasions I have judged for myself".

The weather was still fine, the sea calm, and as far as Harvie-Brown was concerned the skipper was a coward, but there was nothing to be done except to go aboard and regret the missed opportunity.

The "Eunice" sailed away with its naturalists and their "bag" of bird specimens and eggs. Harvie-Brown quickly recovered from his disappointment and enjoyed the voyage back to Stornoway on a beautiful night. He was very pleased with himself:

124

"Stayed up late on deck, talking and joking with the men, singing snatches of songs, and very pleased with our visit to 'Rona — Queen of the gems of the Sea'. All our men — a capital crew — quite as pleased as ourselves, in their own way".

As they approached Stornoway the rain came on.

Harvie-Brown decided that sometime he would return to the island with Norman MacLeod and stay at least three or four days. He had the whimbrels in mind, and also wished to explore the "slanting pit which is situated on the Narrow Neck of land which forms an isthmus between the N and S parts of Rona". He had seen the circular hole falling "some 80 feet" into the dark, and had marked it on his hurried sketch with an arrow. "It looks a dangerous place for man or beast and ought to be fenced for the sheep". According to a descendant of Iain Buidhe, this hole was burst out from below by the sea roaring into Sgeildige on the night of 18th December 1862 when six Ness boats were lost. It is possible to climb down to the round wet boulders at the back of the Sgeildige cave, and look out to the daylight and the incoming waves.

R.M. Barrington, a botanist, camped on Rona for two days, 29th June to 1st July 1886, and was kept awake at night by the noise of the petrels in the village ruins. Other than comments on the very large number of gulls and puffins, and on the black guillemots breeding in the walls of the old houses, he gave very little information about his brief stay, though he did provide the first list of island plants.

Then, a year later, in the very fine summer of 1887, Harvie-Brown made his second visit, this time in his own yacht, the "Shiantelle". In the company of Professor Heddle, a geologist, and Mr Norrie, whose task was to take photographs, he came in to Geodha Stoth and landed at three o'clock in the afternoon of 18th June with even greater ease than on the visit of 1885. Norman MacLeod was possibly with the party as a "pilot".

Straightaway Harvie-Brown, eager to see if the whimbrels were nesting, made off over the thrift and stones of Fianuis but found no trace of them. Oystercatchers were abundant however:

"Desiring fresh meat on board the yacht, Harvie-Brown was induced to add eight of these birds to the larder, which was accomplished in a few minutes. He could just as easily have doubled the number, but disliked the job".

When cooked properly, he said, they tasted like teal duck. From Fianuis the visitors turned their attention to other parts of the island previously unexplored.

"After some biscuits and potted meat, and a pull at Silver's water-bottle, Heddle and I climbed the eastern top of Ronay, 355 feet, but mist obscured the view. We then crossed over the green valley and slope facing the south, and so along the second hillside to the ruins of the old village . . . In the ruined masonry of the old church we heard the churring of the Fork-tailed Petrels . . . but a desecrating blow from the doctor's hammer upon some garnet-holding lump of rock silenced their revelry, and they stopped".

Having frightened the petrels, they walked on, round by the cliffs of Tòn Breighe, and were excited to see fulmars which had been first recorded at Rona by Barrington the year before, but they were disappointed at not finding a nest.

Next day, 19th June, they landed again, "principally to allow of photographs being taken", and the man with the camera, Mr Norrie, "was successful in obtaining several fine views". One of these views is the first known photograph of the chapel and graveyard; the walls of the chapel appear uncollapsed, the vegetation is low enough to reveal many gravestones, and Harvie-Brown, dressed in a kind of yachtsman's uniform, lies on the ground with Heddle beside him. Most interesting of all, the three-holed stone cross stands in line with the chapel doorway, still perhaps in its original position. No stone yet marks the grave of Malcolm MacDonald and Murdo MacKay. In the evening on the same quiet day the "Shiantelle" moved over to Sula Sgeir, where Heddle and Harvie-Brown landed "with perfect ease". Then they sailed away with their Rona trophies, among them Mr Norrie's photographs, the shot oystercatchers, and the three fork-tailed petrels with the six petrel eggs kept after another hour's digging in the village.

Harvie-Brown was a naturalist, collector, and at the same time a recorder of events. His book, published in 1888, contains his observations on wild life, and what he could find out about some of the places he visited. On the subject of Rona, he quotes the old accounts, gives a version of Alexander Carmichael's information on the fate of the two shepherds, and describes his own explorations. This mixture of topics makes his writings yet another contribution to the history of the island. Later visitors whose main interest was in natural history but who also felt that information about Rona and their own adventures in getting there was worth recording found his example difficult to follow. Because most of what they said was a repetition and quotation they did not add much that was new to the Rona story. It is necessary therefore to give only a brief account of some of the more notable visits and events.

Before the first world war the adventurous Duchess of Bedford made four landings on Rona from her steam yacht.[190] She found that "hundreds of fulmars" were present, many nesting in the ruined village and elsewhere away from the cliffs; in 1914 she noted far fewer in the ruins, the result she thought of recent interference by "two gentlemen" who "had put up a shelter in one of the houses" for a few

The graveyard and chapel, Rona, a photograph taken in 1887 showing the three-holed stone still in what was probably its original situation. J.A. Harvie Brown lies on the left.

(photo. see Harvie Brown & Buckley opp. p. 154)

127

days. She was very scornful of the "horrible modern" tombstone which had been erected over the grave of the two shepherds and recently whitewashed. The 1914-18 war put Rona out of bounds although one or two local visits were made, and among other naval activity in the area the "Sappho" was sent to search the island when it was rumoured that the enemy might be using it as an aircraft base. "She reported, after examination, that the island was, as expected, unsuitable for such a purpose". There were minefields around Rona, and enemy submarines. In June 1917 five Dutch fishing boats were attacked by submarines near Rona, and three were sunk. The crews got into small boats, one of which managed to reach Cunndal while the two others were guided into Stoth by the fishing boat "Thelma" whose skipper was Alexander Morrison of Fivepenny.[191] "Thelma", a sgoth built by Murdo MacLeod, was registered in 1916 and after the war passed to John MacIver grocer in Swainbost who sold her to a Skigersta crew. She was renamed "Peaceful". In 1924 representatives of the Royal Commission on Ancient and Historical Monuments arrived on Rona to look at the remains of human occupation. The cross with the three holes was still there, but "There is evidence that private parties landing from yachts have not scrupled to interfere with ancient monuments and even to remove such as were portable".[192] In this way St. Ronan's cell, Iain Buidhe's house, and the place where Malcolm MacDonald and Murdo MacKay are buried, were turned into "ancient monuments".

Three years later, on 29th July 1927, J. Wilson Dougal, a manufacturing chemist from Glasgow, reached Rona on the steam drifter "Pisces".[193] For many years Dougal had spent his annual holiday in Lewis, during which time he devoted himself to "discovering its true geological formation". These holidays had enabled him to gather information about the island among the Ness villages, and it was doubtless with great impatience that he waited several weeks in Stornoway for conditions that would allow the "Pisces" to make the voyage. There was more than one postponement, but at last the Friday arrived when he and his party were able to set off. Dougal's companions included "Messrs MacLeod, Vipon, Stephen and Woodger", and it was probably the last mentioned who, under the initials J.W., wrote a description of their expedition for the Stornoway Gazette.

The party went on board "full of the thrills of adventure", and Dougal lectured them on what they would see and do. On the way north to Port of Ness they had tea on deck, which meant buns and "biscuits of many varieties", with "one member consuming so many oatcakes that we thought he would be the first to hang over the ship's side and gaze at the rolling waves". However the oatcake enthusiast

Guillemot Cliff.

(photo. Frank Rennie)

"nobly survived". They reached Ness at 7.30 in the evening, and a small boat put out to take the visitors ashore. Butter, eggs and lemonade were purchased at a late open village store. Perhaps with a vivid memory of the discomforts suffered on the sea, J.W. remarked that "The harbour at Ness is a very beautiful sight".

As they were preparing to leave several fishermen wished them a safe return, and "the pilot" asked whether they had plenty of water and food "as we never know what might happen on the voyage northwards. These remarks rather scared some of us". Then "ten sturdy Ness men" embarked as well, the annual sheep clipping crew, and with a total of 21 men on board the "Pisces" left the slightly sheltered waters of Port. A short while later they picked up a small boat "just off the Butt", probably from Stoth, and "This proved a thrilling incident" in the strong swell. Dougal and his friends felt ill, so they lay down and tried to sleep away the journey. Early in the morning there came a shout of "Rona", but it turned out to be Sula Sgeir, so they had to settle down again in the cold and mist, "rolling all over the place".

The "Pisces" came in to Geodha Stoth and anchored. At 7 a.m. nearly everyone went ashore. "The shepherds with their four dogs . . . energetically set out to gather the half wild sheep into the fank, shearing and separating the lambs from the ewes, which were to be taken to Ness." Dougal himself set off with his geological hammer, while the others wandered more casually after collecting insects in pure alcohol "for scientific purposes at Edinburgh". One or two took photographs, while "some of us went after birds — feathered ones", disturbing hundreds of them as they climbed the Tòbha. J.W. was not well acquainted with either the human life or the natural history of the Western Isles. At the village, "Near the Tunnels we found two rough pieces of stone, with holes in the centre and one containing another hole towards the side, and these we took to be some kind of mill stones". Their guesses as to the identity of what were really young fulmars were not so good:

> "In the priest's cell of the church we had rather a novel experience, encountering a queer type of bird, which spat blood and a greyish white fluid with an awful smell. These birds nestled in each of the four corners, and as soon as we lowered ourselves down we came under the fire of these spitfires. So great and accurate were their shots that we had to retreat until we could put stones in front of their beaks to stop them from covering us with their nauseous fluid. They were pure white in colour, and were very fluffy, round in shape, and about a foot in circumference. They had no visible wings, and did not seem inclined to move".

J.W. must have felt they had made a startling discovery for later he added that "A number of birds on this island have no names, and have yet to be examined by experts".

The visitors saw rough crosses in the graveyard and the series of cultivation ridges which they "believed to be the dwellings of men in the Ice Age". Having no time to dig, they could not confirm this latter idea. On the Tòbha they saw a pile of stones which they thought must once have been a beacon. In general they were not greatly interested in heaps of stones, so they went back to the landing place, where the Ness-men "favoured us by killing a lamb, which was broiled over a peat fire, served and eaten with relish . . . With tea, bread, butter, cheese and mutton, there was no lack of provision". J.W. said that "We ate the meat like cannibals with a piece of wire and our fingers".

Dougal saw puffins hauled out from under stones with their beaks firmly clamped to a finger, a customary piece of bird-hunting on the annual sheep visit. He heard stories about Rona, including one in which a party of Ness men, sailing to the island for young puffins, was approached by a French brig. Fulmars are also mentioned, but are not supposed to have been present on Rona at that time. On their going aboard the vessel, they found themselves being addressed by Prince Charles Edward who tried to win their service in support of his cause, but they cautiously refused to agree. Later Dougal received a written version of what was possibly Aonghas Bard's composition:

> "An old song about Rona is sung at ceilidhs in Ness by some of the old people. Friends in Ness have kindly obtained from an old gentleman, eighty years of age, the twelve verses of which the song is composed. Its theme is a shepherding expedition in Rona, and is a poetical report by one of the shepherds recounting the difficulties and trials of the men".

When the clipping and other work was finished and everyone was back on board, the "Pisces" left at about 7.30 p.m. for Stornoway, calling at Port of Ness on the way. The "Rona Annual" was over once again. Dougal and his friends carried away vivid memories:

> "The things that struck us most were the quantity of birds and how tame some of these were, also the greenness of the grass, to say nothing of the clarity of the sea round the shore".

MacFarquhar's half-bred sheep were flourishing. "Such is the richness of the pasture that they are much more prolific", wrote Dougal's daughter Helen in a University dissertation on Lewis the following year; "and it was reported (with pardonable exaggeration) by one of the shearers in 1927 that 15 of the ewes had three lambs, and the rest produced two each".[194]

On the rocky eastern coast of Ness, near Skigersta, stands a stone memorial to Dougal, whose amateur geological pursuits brought him

Guillemots on the Rona cliffs.

(photo. Author's Collection)

a close acquaintance with that district. Most of the naturalists and yachtsmen who followed him to Rona over the next few years paid much less attention to the wealth of local, traditional knowledge among the Ness people.

Malcolm Stewart, like T.S. Muir, managed to express vividly the excitement of an expedition to a remote speck of land in the wide ocean.[195] Stewart, a geology student at the time, made out Rona from the lighthouse tower at Cape Wrath in Sutherland, and twice landed there. In 1930 he and D.M. Reid, who was a science master at Harrow, went ashore at Geodha Stoth from the steam trawler "Sophos", and were left for a five days' camp. They explored the island, found both the old three-holed cross and the shepherds' gravestone — "a hideous modern erection" according to Stewart — and made their records of birds.* For all his quotations however, Stewart added little to the Rona story.**

* The three-holed cross disappeared from Rona in the next year or two but Stewart found that it had been placed in Teampull Mholuadh at Eoropie in Ness.

** In repeating the early information about Rona Stewart filled gaps in the story with completely unfounded statements for which reason his "historical" account is of little use, and apart from the natural history observations, the only facts he added were that about 200 sheep, belonging to Alexander MacFarquhar of Dell, pastured on the island in 1930-31.

132

In July 1936 Robert Atkinson and John Ainslie were landed on the island from the east-coast drifter "Rose", and stayed for nearly a month. They put a rickcloth roof over part of the house which had been occupied by Malcolm MacDonald and Murdo MacKay, and which, for some reason, had been named "the manse" by J. Harvie-Brown. Their main aim was to study the fork-tailed petrels, but they had plenty of time to explore the island. They found quernstones, the corroded mooring-ring on Fianuis, and a clay lamp. When they got back they went on to the Shiants and Canna, and then visited Ness to find out more about Rona. Mrs MacLeod of Ocean Villa, celebrating her eighty-eighth birthday, was very helpful; she told them "the histories of innumerable, indistinguishable MacDonalds and Mac-Leods", and introduced them to a Mr Murdo MacLeod who spoke of his grandfather's life on the island, but they did not make much of the information and unfortunately concluded that "trying to trace records of Rona was certainly easier in the visitors' books than in the field of Ness".*[196]

Frank Fraser Darling and his family made their first camp on Rona in the summer and early autumn of 1938, from 12th July to 30th September. His aim was to study the seals, and had it not been for "the international crisis" in late September he would have stayed on until the end of the year. As it was he unluckily missed the peak period of the seals' breeding season in October and early November but was able to return on 15th November for a further five weeks. His living accommodation was two wooden huts erected within the sheep fank where Leathad Fhianuis begins to level out at the exposed narrow neck above Sgeildige. In case of emergency he raised the walls of a stone hut on Fianuis, and placed a long timber spar over the top to take a tarpaulin.[197] The west wall of the fank was also built up to give added shelter to the huts from the driving spray blown out of Sgeildige on a northwesterly gale, and Darling recorded vividly the storm conditions against which the old Rona people had defended themselves by covering their houses with turf:

"Fianuis becomes an inferno when a big northerly or westerly gale is blowing . . . The water climbs up the steep gullies on the west side of the peninsula and at a height of fifty or sixty feet above the sea has still sufficient force to roll boulders up and down which may weigh anything from a hundredweight to two tons . . . Immense seas break over the cliffs as far as the storm-beach and spray rises twice or thrice the height of the cliffs. The spray breaks the full three hundred feet of height of the western cliffs of Rona in a winter gale and is driven right over the island".

★ Had they been able to give sufficient time and attention to local tradition, they could have discovered more than enough to sort out the families, but they missed their chance. "Personally" wrote Atkinson later, "I could never find such stuff anything but tedious . . ." (1949) p. 156.

Using Mr Norrie's photograph as a guide, Darling spent days in rebuilding the collapsed south wall of the chapel, so that the doorway and small window were restored to something like their original appearance, and they are still more or less complete. He then cleared the floor of the interior, digging away the earth and stones blocking most of the entrance to the cell and uncovering what he called the "altar supports" on either side. He found shell sand below packed clay and on top of paving stones, with a scatter of charred bird and seal bones. Within the cell Darling cleared to the paving inside the door, and exposed the altar to its full height of two and a half feet. At its foot, on the right-hand side, he found a large round polished stone of green serpentine marble. In a search through the village he unearthed "one perfect quernstone 22 inches across which was buried in the floor of the largest dwelling"; this he placed in the west end of the chapel, along with two more whole quernstones from the top of a house wall, several quern fragments dug from around the ruins, and two parts of stone vessels.

In the course of their four wild months on the island, Fraser Darling and his family discovered many of its hidden features, such as the mooring ring at Stoth, and the iron bar in the rock at Caolas Lòba Sgeir. They became familiar with summer rain and winter gales; they saw the cliffs full of birds and Fianuis churned to mud by the breeding seals. When they went back on a calm day in June 1939, the island was its welcoming green. The two huts had somehow survived in the fank and proved a useful shelter again from the wind and cold of the following week. On their day of departure the sea was rough, but by lowering the boxes over the cliff at Sgeildige they managed to take off all their remaining stores. The huts were left and soon were tipped out of the fank by the Ness sheep clipping party. Darling later found the larger one in pieces. War came and a second autumn among the seals was to prove impossible, but no other visitor has had the opportunity to become so well acquainted with Rona.

Wartime undoubtedly brought many an unrecorded stranger to the remote islands of north-west Scotland. There were those who made official visits, and others who survived or died after shipwrecks and plane crashes. St. Kilda still holds the scattered remnants of several planes, but it was on Rona that a plane made a forced landing with happier and no less dramatic results. The story has been told by Robert Atkinson in "Shillay and the Seals":

"On 23rd April, 1941, a Whitley aircraft of No. 612 Squadron took off from Wick, on a practice flight over the Atlantic. Wing Commander J.B.M. Wallis, commanding the squadron, was captain and pilot. For purposes of the exercise he decided to turn on Rona but as he reached the island an oil pipe fractured in the port engine. The cumbersome secret equipment under each wing made the aircraft very difficult to fly on one engine. There was a roaring east wind and a high sea; the aircraft was already losing height; in the few seconds left for a decision the captain chose to land on Rona".

It appears that this was not the first time that Wing Commander Wallis had had to make such a decision. In this instance the only other alternatives were to come down in the sea or make a futile flight towards Wick, and the choice was inevitably Rona. The plane came in from the west against a wind that helped to reduce its speed and landed safely on top of the island with no one hurt, little damage, and a wireless transmitter still working. Within four hours an Air Sea Rescue launch arrived from Kirkwall and the survivors went aboard. The launch sheltered overnight in the lee of the cliffs and returned next morning to Thurso. A secret salvage operation was then mounted in order to recover the aircraft and its special equipment. The trawler "Preston North End" landed a party within a few days, and by the first evening "tents, food, water, arms, W/T gear and even carrier pigeons" had been brought safely ashore. The trawler left, and the Flight Sergeant in charge, D.C.F. Waller, made the old village the party's headquarters. The dismantling of the aircraft and the man-handling of the parts down to the cliff edge on sledges took a fortnight. With the aid of a running chain hoist on a steel cableway all the sections were safely loaded on a lighter in three days. The operation was complete, and the aircraft even flew again. But this was not the end of the story. Flight Sergeant Waller told how the party had become interested in the old ruined walls of the houses:

> "it was whilst exploring these in an endeavour to satisfy our curiosity we found the mummified remains of a human being. Except for a few mouldering scraps of clothing there was no means of identification, we could only assume that he was a seafaring man who had made the island after his ship had been torpedoed. Had crawled into the shelter of the ruins and died of starvation or exhaustion . . . This was reported to the Naval Authorities but when I left after my stay of twenty days his blackened remains still lay curled in a cranny in the stonework".[198]

Flight Sergeant Waller's account must be as near the truth as anyone can now get. Unfortunately various other versions were put around afterwards; according to one the salvage party found a skeleton at the summit cairn on the Tòbha where they buried it, while another states that a trawler was sent either to fetch away the remains or bury them. In July 1949 Dr I. Pennie went ashore from a yacht and in crawling through a passageway in the ruins happened to come upon a dessi-cated hand jutting up from the earth floor. Three years later the

Smiths, camping on Rona for a week, found a human skull in a crevice and buried it in the graveyard wall. Mrs Smith gave details which were reported in the "Glasgow Herald",[199] and later in the "Orcadian".[200] After the appearance of the latter, the "Sunday Express" followed up "this mystery of the North Rona, a hump of peat and rock", and provided yet another version of the discovery which had been told to Dr Robert Morrison, who had visited Rona in his yacht.[201] Dr Morrison gave a lift one day to a stranger who claimed to have been in the salvage party and who told how after a few days in the camp a shift of wind brought a powerful stench like that of a dead sheep. Upon investigating, the party came on the body of a German naval officer in No. 1 uniform with hat on, sitting upright against a hut wall. There were no identity papers or disc, nothing to indicate how he came to be there, and, being in the decaying state that it was, the body was buried in the hut floor. Naturally the paper made the most of this, even though it appears to have been almost entirely made up. When Mrs Smith was back on Rona in 1958 the turf on the graveyard wall and the skull which had been placed under it were both gone.

A great skua diving over the grass on Rona's ridge.

(*photo. Ian Bone*)

PART IV

AFFECTIONS OF THE NESS
PEOPLE

Seals and Sheep

Yachtsmen, naturalists and others have continued to visit Rona from time to time, and in June 1956, the island, with its only neighbour, Sula Sgeir, became a National Nature Reserve. Subsequent management of the islands by the Nature Conservancy Council, with its concern for the seabirds and seals, marks an important stage in the course of events, but it is a step aside from the main route where St. Ronan, the Murrays, the MacKays and the rest are to be found. The interest of all visitors, from the minister Donald Morison to today's conservationists and writers, stands inevitably at some distance from the historical ties between Rona and Ness. After all, the descendants of Fionnlagh Ruadh, Iain Buidhe, Murchadh Ban and Alasdair Mac Ruairidh are still living in all the Ness villages.

After the departure of the last family in the late 1830s corn and potatoes were no longer grown in Rona, but it was still possible to take from the island the different kind of annual crop provided by seals, birds and sheep. These did not require daily care so much as occasional visits, sometimes, as in the case of the seals especially, at risky times of the year.

The drowning in Poll Heallair early in the eighteenth century took place when the men of the island were hunting seals, a custom which their ancestors must also have practiced for seal skins and blubber were invaluable to survival on Rona. The blubber was heated and rendered down to oil, and it is said that a piece was commonly hung from the roof above the fire so that the oil dripped into the smouldering turf and produced flames, with their greater heat and cheerfulness. Iain Buidhe recollected how he killed seals in the autumn breeding season and used seal oil probably as well as cuddie oil for his cruisgean, the clay or metal hanging lamps once used in the Hebrides. The large boat sent out by the Murrays in the summertime came back with island produce that included oil, and Alexander Carmichael heard that the crew might pay a small amount "for the privilege of killing seals" during a stay on the island which could last a week or perhaps much more. Since it occurred during the summer months this form of seal hunting must, like that long before at Poll Heallair, have taken place among the caves and creeks, for at that season the seals were not ashore for breeding and only came out of the water to rest and sleep on ledges and outlying rocks. There is a tradition that at one time it was believed that there were no seals on Rona, but that long after, a Harrisman, Aonghas mac Fhionnlaigh na Hearadh, said he was sure seals were breeding in Fianuis.*[202]

* Aonghas was married to a Ness woman.

It may be that hunting itself, and the presence of people all the year round, kept down the numbers, and that after 1850 when disturbance was less likely the breeding colony increased, but this is not certain. In the 1880s the seven casks of oil gathered by Malcolm MacDonald and Murdo MacKay show that seals were still being killed, and Harvie-Brown had more to say on this practice. Pointing out that there was a tradition of seal-hunting at remote rocks and small islands such as Hasgeir and Gasgeir, he remarked that "perhaps the two most important localities" were Rona and Sulasgeir to which expeditions were made "almost annually" by Ness fishermen. He found it difficult to be precise about numbers killed because he was given conflicting information, but he had been told by Norman MacLeod, Ness, of fourteen men killing 360 in 1882 and 230 in October 1883. In a letter R.M. Barrington informed Harvie-Brown that he had questioned the Ness men individually, the skin-buyer, John Morrison, and J.N. Anderson, the "Danish Consul" in Stornoway who dealt with the skins and blubber, but "not two of them agreed". The actual hunters differed among themselves. John Morrison, who received the produce from the Ness men, gave 107 from Rona in 1883, 143 in 1884, and 89 in 1885, while Anderson wrote to Barrington on 24th July 1886 that for the past few years he had received from Morrison "most of the skins of the seals killed on Ronay or Sulisgeir, and their number has been from 120 to 150".[203]

Writing a letter from Ocean Villa on 17th December 1885 Mrs MacLeod reported on the local sealing expeditions. "Indeed since I last wrote you", she began, and she had written to the same correspondent on 30th November and 1st December, "one of our local boats left here on a Friday morning and returned next night with 95 seals which they killed on Rona". She then described the usual arrangements: "One or two boats go from here every November to kill the seals . . . They sometimes kill over two or three hundred seals, they sell them to a local fish curer [probably John Morrison, Lionel] who gets oil made from the blubber and sends it to the southern markets, the skins are nearly all sold in Stornoway. Some gentlemen used to buy a few skins and send them south to be made into vests, coats, aprons, mats and so on. The skins of those who were killed lately are still in Ness, and if you would care to have one for a vest, I will be glad to purchase one for you and send it by parcel post". Mrs MacLeod added thanks for an invitation to call if she happened to be in Edinburgh — "I was in Edinburgh *for a few hours* eleven years ago".[204]

A club was used for killing the seals, and this was sometimes the falamadair — tiller — of the boat, which might be five or six feet long.* It was important to swing the club directly overhead with both

* An axe might also be used.

hands for otherwise even a young seal might seize the club in its teeth and either wrench it out of the hands or by a twist swing the fisherman over a rock. Three or four men could kill scores of seals in a few hours; they pushed the dead ones into the sea, from which they were hauled into boats waiting nearby.[205] The total quantity to be killed depended on the number of boats that could come out, each sgoth having a crew of about 8 or 9 men. It was common for pieces of equipment to be stored under the large boulder on Fianuis near Geodha Stoth, and for the men to sleep under the boat's sail in the fank. If it turned stormy they might have to move over to the village, and it could happen that the return journey was delayed for up to three weeks, in which case the boll of white oatmeal and the potatoes which had been brought out as emergency supplies would be used up, along with a sheep or two killed out of necessity. In return for all this effort and danger each man might finish up about £3 better off.

Usually only one boat went to Rona for seals, and this was generally from Skigersta where first hand knowledge of the hunting expeditions survived as late as the 1970s, though Angus Gunn, a well known hunt skipper before the first World War, was from Lionel. On one occasion at least the boat went out twice to Rona, and additionally to Sule Skerry, in the one season. On his visit in 1927 Dougal was interested in the old Rona village and noted that "In present days the Ness men when sealing spend their nights here, and are disturbed by the twitter of the stormy petrels, which, as darkness comes, leave the sea to spend the night in the ancient stone dwellings".[206] Such disturbance was not likely to be so great in late October or November as in the height of the breeding season for the birds in July and August. Dougal also pointed out that tragedies occurred, and he mentioned a boat full of Ness sealers that was lost at sea, though he does not say when this happened. He also described an incident with a happier outcome, which locally is considered to have happened in the stormy November of 1914 and to have been the last seal expedition.*

"During the Great War a number of Ness men proceeded on a sealing expedition to Rona. As fears for their safety had arisen by their non-appearance, a request was made to the authorities to investigate. A small cruiser was sent and sailed round the island, but saw no trace of the men. The report of the cruiser caused great grief amongst the assembled people at Ness Harbour. The cruiser returned to Oban. Some time later a trawler reported having seen men moving on the island. The cruiser again went to Rona and found the men, who, owing to the storms, had sheltered themselves about the island, and had not seen the first appearance of the cruiser. Thus joy came to the Ness people to find their men again".[207]

* In 1912 the boats Eathar Gheddy and Eathar a' Bhàird, from Eoradale and Skigersta, went to Rona for seals and were stranded there for many weeks in bad weather.

It is also maintained that the sealers were proud enough not to want the cruiser on its first visit to find them, and that on the second occasion, when they were being taken off, the seal hunt skipper refused at first to leave his boat and the seals that had been killed.

On arrival in Ness the skins, with the blubber adhering, were processed or sold, and, if a whole seal was brought back, the meat was eaten. Ness opinion was not recorded, but in 1867 Alexander Carmichael went into a house on Heisgeir, the Monach Isles, where a young seal was being cooked. "I tasted the flesh", he said, "and it was very agreeable. The flavour was not unlike that of venison". Blubber could also be eaten, as Carmichael described:

'A stripe of blubber about one inch wide was cut along the back of the seal. This was laid on a table and a board with some weight laid on the top. After lying in this position till much of the oil was pressed out, the edges on each side were thinly paired [i.e. pared] and the pairings thrown into the melting pot. The pressed blubber was then cut into convenient bits and eaten with bread".[208]

However most of the blubber, cut off the skin with a knife, was put into the "melting pot", a large cast iron cauldron, and heated over peat fires. The oil so produced was a clear golden fluid, strained into bottles for storage and used as a medicine for ailments such as asthma. As for the skins, whether they were sold or kept at home, they were turned into items of clothing; in Ness a favourite product was the spliuchan — tobacco pouch.

The November voyages for seals were at the mercy of the weather, and the open sailing boats that went to Rona, such as "Challenger" and "Charlie Orrock", of typical Ness sgoth design, were always at risk. Peats for the fire provided some ballast on the outward journey, and for the return there were the skins and blubber at least. In bad weather whole seals were brought back as they helped to keep the water out. On more than one occasion, while the men were ashore, the wind turned fiercely into the north, driving the sea onto both sides of Fianuis, so that the boat had to be taken up on land; and homeward journeys were often made hazardous when they were forced upon the crew by incoming rough weather with rapidly rising gales which could swing across the compass and move from north or west into the southeast, bringing great seas to prevent progress towards the Butt.

The work involved in dealing with the sheep on Rona was easier in so far as it did not involve winter journeys, but it too had its difficulties and dangers.

From earliest recorded times sheep had been kept on Rona. Wool and ewes' milk cheese always formed part of the rent, and grain and meal had been sent to Ness in sheepskin bags. The Reverend Donald

Morison's party was provided by the Rona people with five newly killed sheep, and, only a few years before, the account of Rona received by Sir Robert Sibbald had mentioned that the wool was "of a bluish colour" as if this indicated some distinctive feature of the type of animal on the island. Both cattle and sheep were an important feature of the Murrays' farming arrangements, and, after the disappearance of the old community one of the main tasks of the shepherd/crofter families continued to be the care and management of the stock. MacCulloch found Kenneth MacCagie looking after fifty small sheep, one of which was killed as a gift for the visitor, but it seems that usually the flock was larger than this; Murdo MacDonald recollected that there used to be up to 100 sheep, and Iain Buidhe said that there had been 200 sheep in his day. From that time on when the cultivated land was abandoned and added to the grazing, 200 remained the average figure. This was the number in 1850, and in the early 1880s when Tormod Pìobair was shepherd with 100 sheep of his own.

Harvie-Brown, noting that the sheep continued to suffer "occasional losses from their falling over rocks or being stolen by the crews of passing vessels", was apparently the first to name the breed on Rona. He said of the Murrays that "They usually kept from 100 to 160 sheep of the blackface breed upon it".[209] These must have been the old Lewis type of blackfaced which had developed after the introduction to Lewis of blackface sheep from the mainland at the end of the eighteenth century, and cross-breeding, not well controlled, between blackface rams and the native small Hebridean sheep. The Murrays, as tenants, no doubt took the new breed to Rona, probably in the shape of two rams which would begin the process of change in the existing native flock. Certain native characteristics survived, such as a wild nature and a tendency to scatter when disturbed, but with the arrival of new rams every two years the size and appearance of the old inbred sheep was greatly changed and improved.

In the mid 1880s Finlay MacKenzie succeeded to the tenancy and "keeps a stock of some 200 sheep upon the island". They were of the improved breed, which flourished in the summertime on the varied vegetation of what had always been considered very fertile land. At this time Alexander Carmichael, who seems to have provided Harvie-Brown with a great deal of information about Rona, wrote that MacKenzie's sheep, "like those of similarly outlying islands round the west coast, suffer much from the depredations of passing vessels and of English smacks fishing in their neighbourhoods".[210] However, in 1888 Farquhar Murray, who had just taken over, was so pleased with the stock that he tried some on Sula Sgeir:

1947. Sheep stream off up the west side of Leathad F hianuis above the gathering pen. Those in the middle of the line are crossing the curve of a length of wall not easily noticed on the ground.

(photo. Robert Atkinson)

143

"I endeavoured to use the Island of Sulisker for grazing purposes and accordingly transferred 24 of the purest class of lambs from Rona to that of Sulisker, where they thrived exceedingly well during the month of August and realized a head more than those I brought ashore at the same time. I also left seven tup lambs in Sulisker during the winter and found them the following summer in first class condition".[211]

So, in spite of the sea journeys, accidental losses and theft, the tenant evidently felt that Rona and even Sula Sgeir were more than worthwhile as sheep pastures.

The Murray blackfaces were still on Rona after the first World War. Between 1914 and 1920 access to the island was severely restricted, and the sheep became wilder than usual. They were of course theoretically subject to the laws of dipping, but in their isolation were eligible for exemption provided that any that were moved were dipped before they went to the island or within three days of being taken off it. An episode during the war reveals in few words much that was involved in keeping sheep on Rona at this time.

On 16th February 1917 the Stornoway Gazette reported a "Peculiar Case Relating to Sheep". Donald Murray of 5 North Dell, Donald Weir of Swainbost (represented by his son) and Donald Gunn of 19 North Dell appeared before the Sheriff in Stornoway accused of contravening the Sheep Dipping Order. The complaint against the three crofter tenants was that as joint owners of 35 sheep on "North Rona Island" they had failed to get them dipped. On behalf of the men, Mr Anderson lodged a plea of not guilty, saying that since 1914 they had been unable to get a boat and an application to the Admiralty for one of its ships had been unsuccessful. Moreover, when last there in 1914, they had had a remarkable adventure. They had taken off 50 sheep (in a sgoth) but were caught in a gale on the homeward voyage and had been forced to run before the wind as far as Loch Eriboll in Sutherland where the boat was wrecked. The crew and the sheep managed to reach the shore safely, and almost immediately the sheep were sold. The men then walked all the way to Kyle of Lochalsh, where they managed to hitch a lift on a patrol boat home to Stornoway. Now, in 1917, they did not even know if there were sheep on Rona. The Sheriff observed, apparently in connection with nothing in particular, "There's nobody living on Rona". The procurator fiscal accepted the facts, sympathised with the tenants, but pointed out that they had failed to apply for exemption after being told that they could do so by the local constable. Although they claimed they never knew about exemption, the three men pled guilty and were fined 5/– each on condition that they now applied.

After the war the annual visits to clip the sheep, with one of which Muir had coincided in 1860 and which had been going on for an

144

c1922. MacLeod's boat 'Eoropie', a converted 'Fife' fishing boat formerly called the 'Olive Branch', about to leave the harbour at Port of Ness for Rona. About a dozen sgothan Niseach lie side by side nearby.

(photo. John Murdo MacLeod Collection)

unknown number of years before that, resumed once again. The dangers were still present, even with the arrival of more solid transport in the shape of the big two sailed boat with a Swedish engine added and nearly fifty feet in length, which Donald Macleod used for bringing supplies of groceries and meal from Stornoway to his shop in Eoropie. This boat, called the "Eoropie", operated from Port, and with Angus MacDonald of Port as skipper went several times to Rona, but in 1928 or 1929 it broke its moorings in the Port harbour, and, partly submerged, was carried by the sea to Orkney where it was recovered and put to use again, though it never came back to Ness. It was possibly this boat to which Dougal referred when he wrote of how, for the annual clipping visit, "Some years ago a large motor-boat was employed and reached Rona in five hours. The return passage was made in eleven hours in a life-and-death struggle with heavy seas".[212] Then, from the late 1920s until the second World War, the usual means of travelling to Rona was one of the steam drifters belonging to the Cunninghams of Scalpay, Harris.

Donald Gunn died in 1924, Donald Murray two years later, and Donald Weir, the third sharer, naturally felt less inclined to continue. It was in these circumstances that Alex MacFarquhar took on the main tenant position and further altered the sheep stock. Before 1910 another breed, the cheviot, was becoming established in Ness, and when a new Murray family went to Swainbost farm in 1908 there was already a mixture of cheviot and blackface there — whitefaced with horns and looking like Welsh Mountain sheep. On Rona the blackface remained until Alex MacFarquhar took over in 1926-27. He then introduced the cheviot by taking rams out and achieving what was already at Swainbost a horned whiteface cross. By pursuing this policy and bringing in replacement rams every two years so as to avoid inbreeding, MacFarquhar managed in a short while to produce a cheviot from which the horns had almost entirely vanished. Inbreeding did occasionally occur when a ram that should have been removed could not be found or caught and this led to deformities. The mating between rams and ewes was of course not controlled by a shepherd, and as a consequence lambs were born from March to June, but this was not an important matter if no sheep were removed for two years. MacFarquhar made a point of choosing new rams from mainland stocks because good local cheviots were not commonly available, but sometimes he would put a black ram on the island and find many black offspring as a result.

At one time, perhaps in the early 1900s and into the 1914-18 war, it is said that few or no sheep were taken out to Rona, and that only the excess of the native breeding flock was brought away. For the most part, however, the annual visit in MacFarquhar's time was planned to

146

achieve a variety of essential good farming work within not much more than twelve hours. The boat left on a convenient but fairly unpredictable day, as early as June in some years, as late as September in others, depending on the weather, availability of a boat or other necessary business. It took with it the new rams, some lambs, and, in the days of the drifters in the 1930s, a small flat-bottomed craft known as "the punt". The punt had been made by John MacLeod (Iain Mhurdo), the Port of Ness boat-builder, specially for ferrying sheep between the drifter and the shore, because the drifter lifeboats were too small and inconvenient for the job. While an ordinary small boat could take perhaps 6 or 7 sheep at a time, the punt could carry twice that number. Also aboard was all the essential equipment required, including wool shears, wool bags, fencing materials, and provisions for at least two or three days. On arrival at the island reasonably early in the morning work began immediately and abruptly.

On the misty wet morning of Thursday 30th July 1936 Robert Atkinson and John Ainslie were woken suddenly by Alex MacFarquhar and his assistants setting out on their first task of gathering the sheep.[213] The "Cailleach Oidhche", a paraffin engined drifter, was at anchor off Geodha Stoth, "her wet-darkened deck no doubt slippery with fish scales and sheep dung, and swilling with dirty water as she rolled". Already provisions and equipment were stowed in the fank, out of sight of the sheep which being "very wild" would shy away from a strange object such as a jacket left lying over a stone. The men from the boat had set off with dogs up Leathad Fhianuis and spread out round the shores and cliff edges of the south part of the island, moving with shouts and waves to drive all the sheep down the slope and right out beyond the fank onto Fianuis. Sometimes sheep would jump off the rocks into the sea and swim away; as many as thirteen were seen once to do this, until, a good distance out from the shore, they tired and began to go round in a circle which meant they were about to drown. Rescue was made difficult by the weight of the waterlogged fleece which meant that the boat might capsize as a sheep was being hauled aboard. In 1936 the sheep gathered out on Fianuis without attempts to swim away.

While they were out there, the fencing was brought into action. The entrance to the fank faces to Fianuis through a gap in the old stone wall that runs across from Sgeildige to Stoth. Fence posts were put up and a wire net funnel made, spreading from the fank entrance to the wall. Fishing nets, and, later, rylock netting were used to the same purpose on other occasions. When the funnel was ready the sheep were slowly driven back from Fianuis. On this 1936 July morning they broke the fences in a forward surge, as they often did, and rushed away up Leathad Fhianuis, so that the whole procedure had to be

c1952. Most of the sheep to be taken off Rona are already aboard. The few still to go are kept under watchful eyes in the pen on Leathad Fhianuis.
(photo. James MacGeoch)

repeated. The second time it was successful, and they packed into the fank, wedged so closely together that there was scarcely room for even a small attempt to jump over the fank wall, and in any case the sheep were tired and heavy fleeced. Forty of their number were thought to be missing since last year's count which might be explained by theft or gales that blew sheep into the sea. The work of clipping and castrating began, the cast ewes and last year's wethers being taken down to the punt as they were ready. As usual "a lamb was killed and put to cook in an iron cauldron over some lumps of coal against the fank wall". Sheep fresh from Rona pasture were considered by some to be not very pleasant to eat, for the flesh had a strong wild taste which in those that were taken to Ness only faded gradually after a few weeks of different grazing. John MacLeod back in Port of Ness would generally get half a lamb for the use of his punt.

As the day progressed the weather worsened, and there were doubts whether the boat could leave that night. Alex MacFarquhar thought that they should wait till the sea went down for sheep might be washed overboard or drowned on deck. At 4.30 a.m. on Friday 31st July the drifter left and had a rough nine hour voyage back to Ness. One year the passage took fifteen hours, with six sheep drowned in the boat on the way. Angus MacKay of Portvoller, in the "Frigate Bird", had to prepare to leave in worsening weather with everyone still ashore, so he sent a message that anybody who wished to get back to Stornoway would have to go out by line through the sea. No-one accepted the offer. Instead the skipper sent sealed tea chests of provisions ashore by the line, and the sheep party settled down to sleep in the fank on the sacks of wool. About 1 a.m. with the rain driving down they moved over to the village for a little more shelter. Then the boat came back in, and with men and sheep aboard set off on the rough journey home. In 1936 Mrs MacLeod, Ocean Villa, well into her eighties but a lively Ness news writer for the Gazette, did not make much of the bad weather in her comment on 7th August:

"Visit to Rona. The drifter 'Cailleach Oidhche' (the Owl) left the Break-water, Port-of-Ness, on Wednesday, 29th inst., at 10 p.m., with Mr A. MacFarquhar (lessee of Rona), his men, lambs, dogs, and other require-ments, for their annual visit to Rona for the purpose of shearing, counting, and otherwise looking after the sheep which are wintering there. It was quite nice weather when they left the Breakwater, but they had not gone far when we heard the foghorn at the Butt blowing. We then felt sure the weather conditions were not favourable. However, the 'Cailleach Oidhche' got back to the Breakwater about 1 p.m. on Friday, the 31st inst., having accomplished the work she set out to do. It was a relief to see the drifter and all safely back, for the 'Rona Annual' has always been considered locally a precarious trip".

The year before the "Rona Annual" had been a much quieter affair, according to the report from Ness on 16th August 1935:

> "Visit to Rona. Early on Monday morning, 5th inst., the drifter, 'Rose I', called at Port of Ness, and took on board Mr Alexander MacFarquhar, farmer, South Dell, his shepherd and a number of local men, and various paraphernalia, including lambs and sheep dogs, for Mr MacFarquhar's annual visit to Rona for the purpose of shearing and otherwise attending to the sheep which are wintered on the island. As the trip to this Island is rather hazardous, and absolutely dependent on the weather, whenever men, etc., are landed on Rona, 'expedition' is the word to use. On Monday the sea was 'like a painted ocean', and the 'Rose I' accomplished the journey to Rona and back within twenty-four hours. With all the work they set out to do, done and finished, Mr MacFarquhar and his party landed safely at Port in the small hours of Tuesday morning".

In July 1937 Alex MacFarquhar fixed up the "Provider" for the "expedition". It left Stornoway in the afternoon, collected the sheep party of 12 men and boys with 4 dogs from Port of Ness in the evening, and arrived off Rona about 4 a.m. The sheep were driven to Fianuis where they stayed for five hours while the wall was repaired and the fence put up. A decoy sheep was tethered at the fank, and the rest were successfully penned in. The lamb was killed and cooked. Forty or more sheep were loaded, followed by the wool bags and the fencing, and the "Provider" returned to Port of Ness by dusk after an "Annual" that was uneventful, much like that of 1935.[214]

According to Alex MacFarquhar the price for mutton meant that a visit to Rona in 1938 was not worthwhile, but he would of course have to go the following year for the rams would have to be changed and the wethers lost condition if they stayed for three years. In place of the Rona Annual, however, the island birds and sheep were disturbed by the arrival by fishery cruiser of Fraser Darling with his family and the sectional huts.[215]

Not long after settling in, on the morning of 2nd August, Darling sighted the smoke of a ship heading in the direction of Rona and after a while it was possible to make out through the telescope that "she was rather more fancy than a trawler, having a large bridge and boats on davits". Further than that, she had "a cumbersome sort of boat hanging from a derrick forward".

It turned out that the vessel was the fishery research ship "Explorer" on her way from Orkney to St. Kilda, where she arrived four days later and brought news of Fraser Darling to Robert Atkinson, then on Hirta. The thing hanging from the derrick was what Darling called an "old flat-bottomed coble", but was to Ness people John MacLeod's punt. The Explorer's captain said that he had picked it out of the sea twenty-five miles east of Rona. "It is a danger to shipping", he said,

Taking sheep off Rona, shortly after 1945. The handlers include: Alasdair MacDonald (Alasdair Beag Dhomhnaill Alasdair Dholaigean), John MacLeod (Iain a Gheàdsear), Donald MacLeod (Domhnall Iain Mhurchaidh).

(photo. Swainbost Farm Collection)

"but rather than sink her we thought it might be useful to you as firewood". Darling then realised that only three days before he had seen the punt pass by Rona from north-west to south-east, about a mile offshore. It had drifted by at a rate of about a mile an hour. "She will do for more than firewood", Darling said. "What about using her as a roof for a storage hut?". The leaking punt was towed in by a launch and was nearly lost at the rocks. After attaching a rope to a ring in the floor, water was baled out, and with considerable effort the punt was brought to the fank and turned over so that the gunwale rested on a low part of the dyke. Darling knocked the stern and thwarts out, and used the little boat as a store for tools and tins of food. His hens and later the seals used it as a shelter also.

In the winter after his return to the mainland Darling wrote to Alex MacFarquhar and mentioned the boat. MacFarquhar replied saying "it must be the one from Ness which had broken its moorings back in the summer. He said it was the one they used to take behind the big sailing-boat years ago when sheep were more regularly taken to and from Rona". Darling did not think this could be the same boat, but the tale was accepted in Lewis and newspapers made something out of the story of a boat which made its own way home to Rona. In Ness there is a version which states that the punt broke loose on a Sunday in December 1938 and travelled off to the island on its own. Whatever might have been the attitudes at the time, confirmation that it was indeed John MacLeod's punt at the Rona fank came in the summer of 1939, when the next annual sheep visit took place in early August.

Alex MacFarquhar arranged for the drifter "Comrade", with a skipper from Tolsta. On the way from Stornoway to Ness the boat was disabled when the water pump broke down and had to be towed back to Stornoway. Eventually it set off again, and leaving Port of Ness about 8.30 on the evening of 2nd August made for Rona. The sheep party included the young Murdo Murray, his brother-in-law Donald MacLeod, and John Murray, also from North Dell, whose family had left Swainbost farm in 1922.

John Murray had been to Rona in 1929 when he was 15. He would have been there a year before when he was doing odd jobs for MacFarquhar, but his father refused to go if his son did, so the son did not make the journey. When he arrived in 1929 he found a tent at the fank, with camping gear and cooking utensils, but there was no sign of any person on the island. Going again in 1939 he helped to patch the small boat on board with canvas during the voyage, and in the early morning he kept look out for land, which the skipper thought was straight ahead but which he felt was over the port bow. Soon Rona appeared to port. They went first to Sula Sgeir where they landed Robert Atkinson and John Ainslie by the repaired boat about 5 o'clock, and then moved off to Rona. One of the first things that met John Murray's eyes as he came ashore was the up-turned boat left by Darling at the fank. John MacLeod's punt was in Rona still. The party removed it to the rocks, and launched it, but, as it had at least two cracks in it, it sank. They dragged it ashore again, and patched it with pieces of felt that had been left in rolls on the island by Darling. It was put back into the water and then was used for four or five ferrying journeys between shore and drifter but it sank again and went into one of the caves near Geodha Mèadhar where it was left to the sea.

When some loose furnishings had been cleared, Fraser Darling's huts were rolled out of the fank, and the usual hectic gathering of sheep began. An easterly swell had delayed landing, work started late, and the ferry loads of sheep out to the Comrade could not begin until 9 in the evening when the sea had gone down enough to allow use of Geodha Stoth. So it was after midnight on 4th August before Rona was left behind, but the return voyage via Sula Sgeir was made on a fine summer morning — the second last homeward voyage from Rona for Murdo Murray, "the quiet, likeable Murdo" as Robert Atkinson remembered him after the war which so soon followed the "Rona Annual" of 1939.

In the course of the second World War there were two visits to Rona by naval trawler, and the well-fed sheep bore fleeces that grew continually for two or even three years without breaking away. One ram carried a fleece of 22lbs, almost a stone. The wool was very oily and generally better than that produced by the sheep of Ness. The north-country cheviot flock on the island still numbered about 200, and consisted of the latest two rams, young wethers, and breeding ewes from which the oldest were taken away. The number of old ewes removed varied according to the death level and the state of their teeth; if the front teeth were good and firm a ewe might be left another year. Good ram lambs were not "cut" but taken off the island to be sold in Stornoway as rams, and the wethers together with the best ewe lambs were also brought back to Ness. During the war about 100 sheep were removed on each visit. A passing trawler occasionally stole a sheep or two, and evidently guns were used as some live lambs were found to be full of shot.

Sheep brought back from the island were not clipped before they left. For the first two or three weeks in Ness they lost condition, even if in the best fields, and their meat then was not to everyone's taste. They retained their wildness for a long time and would not mix with other sheep. Those for sale were driven to Stornoway, leaving Ness early and spending a night at Barvas. On one occasion it is remembered, after a 5 a.m. start from Ness and the Barvas break, the Rona sheep were going on to Stornoway when they caught up with a flock of

A ram on Rona with a fleece weighing 22-23 lbs, the growth of three or four years. Taken about 1950 the photograph shows four of the 'Rona Annual' group from Ness — (l.-r.) John MacKenzie MacLeod (Iain Sparaig Sneagain), Colin Campbell (Cailean an Irish), John MacKenzie (Nounaidh Tod), Donald Morrison (Domhnall Murdo na casag).

(photo. James MacGeoch)

c1950. A Roma ram led by Angus Morrison (Aonghas Sheumais), Norman Campbell (Tormod na Duic) and John MacKenzie (Nounaidh Tod).
(photo. James MacGeoch)

Point sheep which they passed without a glance. Their distinctiveness was also betrayed in the homing instinct, which many sheep possess. One ram sold to Carloway disappeared and turned up again at Bilisclettir on the way to Cuiashader and Skigersta in Ness, while a group that escaped from Dell Farm made their way to a point near the Butt lighthouse and would no doubt have reached Rona if there had been dry land in between.

The war past, Alex MacFarquhar found it increasingly difficult to arrange a boat for the Annual. Loss of three days fishing meant that skippers were reluctant to go, and if they agreed their charges made the whole sheep enterprise on Rona hardly worthwhile. In July 1946 Robert Atkinson went out in his own boat, and there were the remains of Fraser Darling's huts, lying about by the fank. The following year, with partners again, Alex MacFarquhar's visits revived for a short while; and then the tenancy and the task of the "Annual" passed to the "Queen of the Isles" fishermen. Another stage in the history of Rona had begun.

Sheep packed on the deck of 'Provider', a Stornoway drifter, during the journey from Rona to Lewis in 1937.
(photo. Robert Atkinson)

PART V

THE DISTANT ISLAND

Roma.

160

The Distant Island

The people of Rona, whether of the "ancient race" or of the later solitary families, were closely linked with the communities of Ness. Yet there was something mysteriously different about the earlier inhabitants, with their names and customs that were strange to Lewis, and even Angus Gunn, Fionnlagh Ruadh, Iain Buidhe and the others of only 150 years ago seemed to take on something of that difference merely by living in Rona for a while. In its brown wintery desolation the island was hardly to be imagined somewhere out in the ocean and it was still partially a dream in the green of the summer when the boats would set sail and go there.

No wonder then that there should be stories which float like the island in a world of their own where the sheepskin bags, the drownings, the seals, are to be found beside the saintly Ronan, the headless prince of Lochlann, Luran, and the "cionaran-cròs". Sometimes history enters that strange world, as when the Reverend Donald Morison found himself surrounded by those who had foreseen his coming; and sometimes the Rona world comes to the villages of Ness, in the form of the three-holed cross stone or of Fionnlagh Ruadh returning with his ornament of bone.

On rare occasions one or two of the ancient race of Rona left the island for a while and entered the different world of Lewis or the mainland. For some unexplained reason a Rona man once "had the opportunity of travelling as far as Coul" in easter Ross-shire, where he was astonished by everything he saw; "and when he heard the noise of those who walked in the rooms above him he presently fell to the ground, thinking thereby to save his life, for he supposed that the house was coming down over his head".[216] To him everything was as strange as the arrangement of life on Rona was to any visitor, and as in St. Kilda the world of the island had qualities which were not so easily found across the sea.

In such circumstances quite ordinary events could take on an unusual character or become the subject of a story. From time to time a cuckoo landed on Rona at the beginning of summer; and long ago the loud call of this rare visitor was thought to predict the imminent death of the minister, or of the Earl of Seaforth.[217] The minister himself had cattle on the island, and once when he went there he found two to be missing. He asked the people where they were, and they said one had fallen over "an t-Sìthean" and the other over "Hageir". "Oh yes", the minister answered, "into 'an t-Sìthean' of your belly". Then there were the named ledges of the cliffs: Pala Nighean Ruadh, where a girl used to knit stockings and which she could leave with the aid of a grass rope on the cliff; Pala Chaluim 'ic

1936. Evening light and shadow in the ridges and ruins of the settlement of Roma.

(photo. Robert Atkinson)

162

Fhionnlaigh, where Malcolm MacKay, Fionnlagh Ruadh's son, used to sleep in the days when he was interested in another man's wife and was afraid lest the husband tried to kill him. In more recent times, apparently about the first World War, a dog belonging to Iain Anna Bhàin of South Dell, which was scared when one of the party was shooting birds, was marooned on Rona and mysteriously survived for a period which Dougal said was ten years, and others thought to be one or five. The dog apparently lived off seabirds and possibly carcases of sheep, but not by killing sheep. When found again in the village it was not to be caught, and as it had gone blind it was shot; it is said that the dead dog was so heavy that it took two men to throw her over the cliffs.

So many traces are left of the people and events. The living storehouse of knowledge about them is the memory of a Ness person, and the dead storehouse is the book which tries to take the place of memory. Here and there in the island still or in private houses and museums are the objects which once formed part of Rona life and have not decayed away — the three-holed cross, the round lump of green Iona marble which Fraser Darling found by the altar in the cell, the pieces of undated pottery discovered around the village in 1958, the quern-stones, the oval stone found in the kiln floor with its ends worn by crushing grain, the crusie lamp, the line of stones under the feannagan, the whitewashed gravestone of Malcolm MacDonald and Murdo MacKay. Today Ness is fortunate in its inheritance of the island won for it by the blood of Morrisons centuries ago.

On 16th October 1897 the paper called "The Northern Weekly" carried an article entitled "My First Visit to Ness". The writer had been down to Port of Ness in rough weather:

> "I have stood on the rock above that port in a stiff north easter and have seen the boats coming in of an evening when they could not well live in the open sea much longer with safety. The entrance to the port was through a narrow passage — so narrow that the oars had to be dropped in the sea in the passing, when oars and boats rode in on the billow that surged through. Directly every man jumped into the water as soon as the prow struck the shore, clapped his broad shoulders to the side of the boat and waited the occurring of the next sea to lift her up. The women laid on the painter, and worked with a will in hauling in the boat, as she was gradually lightened of her ballast by the men lifting the slabs of stone on their backs to the shore".

So might a landing from Rona have been watched from the cliff top at Stoth or Cunndal when the Murrays' boat came in or when the Reverend Morison returned with a shilling for a Lewis wife. "These men were brave and knew it not", wrote the same author. Round the peat fire in the evening, when the storm was at its height, he commented on what he had seen. "Oh", came the reply, "that was nothing but an everyday occurrence". The sea journey to Rona, if not everyday, is still accepted as part of the year's pattern, and the guides to the point of the moving horizon where the green island lies somewhere in the ocean are landmarks handed down through generations. By compass the course is "North East a quarter North" — but the marks preserve the link between Ness and Rona: once they were "Cnoc Ard ann an Geodha Chruidh", then "Ath Iain mac Thormoid ann an Geodha Chruidh", and now "Tigh Thormoid an Diùc ann an Geodha Chruidh". They are marks that point not only to a distant island, but to the births and deaths, tales and toil associated with it. "It is with Rona", wrote Dougal, "that the regard and affections of the Ness people are most entwined".

References and Notes

1 *Carmichael Watson Collection* (CWC) University of Edinburgh MS230 Letter from Mrs MacLeod, Ocean Villa, Port of Ness 30 Nov. 1885.
2 *Oban Times* 26 Nov. 1898 Article: "Teampull Ronain" by Rev M. MacPhail, Kilmartin.
3 CWC MS 230 Article: "North Roney" by A. Carmichael.
4 See n.17.
5 See n.58.
6 See p.61.
7 See n.2.
8 R. Campbell *The Father of St. Kilda* London 1901 p.xii.
9 Campbell p.50.
10 A. Carmichael *Carmina Gadelica* 2nd Edit. Edinburgh 1928 Vol. I pp.126-27. Also CWC MS 230 "North Roney". The story is also recorded by MacPhail, and by William Watson (CWC MS 95 pp.48-55) whose version was taken down from Angus Gunn on 20 April 1867:

> "Angus Gunn gives a somewhat different version of this legend. He says Ronan had 2 sisters named respectively Breanil and Mionacan; and he remarks as a great wonder that he never was able to find out how the women got to the island . . ."

> "Theirig gu laimrig Imirstin am maireach agus an each iomchuidh air tighinn. Ach ged a chual Ronan so air feadh na oidhche, cha deach a sios a cheud oidhche, na dara oidhche, ach air an treas fhreagair e an gu thainig an each iomchuidh, tha an each iomchuidh air tighinn. Bha duil aig go faichaidh e bata na eithear an sin, ach cha'n fhaic e ni an sin ach rud mor fada du, ris na chuir e a chas gus an gluasaidh e e A chas a chuir a ri cha b'urrainn e a tharruing air ais, agus mar sin b'eigin dha dol air mulaich na muic, oir se much mhar a bh'ann. Chaidh a mhuic leis gu Rona, agus cha deach deur bùrn air as an aiseag, oir an Ti a thug dha an each iomchuidh, thug e dha aimsir mhaith mar an ceudna. Mar dhearbhadh air so, s'ann air Sronn an Tintinn, a chuir i air tir e, agus se so ait cho gaillionnach 'us a tha s' an eilean. Chan 'eil fhios agam cionnas a fhuair e an dha phiudhar a mach, ach tha teampull Mhiriceil an sud fhathast air bar na bruaich.

> "'Se Flanan brathair Ronain, a bha anns na h-eileanan Flanain, agus se a chreidimh a chuir ann e mar an ceudna, cha ro fhios aig muintir Uig cor son a bha an ainm air na eileannan so gus na dh'innis mise [i.e. Gunn] dhaibhe e. Mar so be Ronan 'us Flanan an da bhrathair, agus Brianil agus Miricil an da phiuthair aca. An uair a thubhairt Ronan ri a phiuthar Brianil, 'Gu ma bhriagh a phearsa a bha aic'. Fhreaghair i nach fhuiraichidh i na b'fhaisg air na far a faicich e cèo a thigh, 'us mar sin b'eigin da tigh a dheanamh di ann an Sulair-sgeir, ach thubhairt Brianil gu fuireachadh ise far a faicidh i e fhein.

> "Cha cual mi e am bàs a chaidh oirre.

> "An uair a chaidh e don eilean bha e làn do bhiastan ach rinn Ronan urnuigh ri Dia agus chur e as iad. Tha ann an sgeirean an eileain fhathast làrachean, sios gu beul na mara, ris an can iad 'Larach nam Biast'".

11 Carmichael (1928) Vol.II p.348.
12 A.O. Anderson & M.O. Anderson (editors) *Adomnan's Life of Columba* London 1961 pp.443, 445.
13 J.F. Webb (trans.) *Lives of the Saints* Penguin Books 1965 p.94.
14 *The Northern Weekly* 30 Sept. 1897. Article: "North Rona and its Seals" by Rev M. MacPhail.
15 R.W. Munro (Editor) *Monro's Western Isles of Scotland and Genealogies of the Clans 1549* Edinburgh 1961 p.88.
16 F. MacLeod (editor) *Togail Tìr: Marking Time* Stornoway 1989 Essay: "A 17th Century Prose Map" by Iain F. MacIver p.27. For Morison's description of Lewis (c1683) see also *Spottiswoode Miscellany* 1845 Vol.II p.339, *MacFarlane's Geog-*

raphical Collections (MGC) National Library of Scotland (NLS) Advocates Manuscript 35.3.12 Vol.II pp.242-47, etc.

17 *Collectanea de Rebus Albanicis* The Iona Club Edinburgh 1847 no.1 "Rentale of the Bishoprick of the Ilis and Abbacie of Ecolmkill" p.4.

18 *Balfour's Collection on the Shires* NLS Advocates Manuscript 33.2.27 f.350.

19 *Sibbald's Collections* NLS Advocates Manuscript 33.5.15 "An Account of the Isles Hirta and Rona given to me by the Lord Register, Sir George MacKenzie of Tarbat, as he had it from intelligent persons dwelling in the place" p.27.

20 For biographical details relating to Rev Donald Morison and his life as minister of Ness and of Barvas see W. Matheson (editor) *An Clàrsair Dall* (The Blind Harper) Scottish Gaelic Texts Society Edinburgh 1970 Appendix G pp.245-46.

21 D.J. MacLeod (editor) *A Description of the Western Isles of Scotland c1695* by Martin Martin (pub. London 1703) Stirling 1934 pp.100-104.

22 Matheson (1970) pp.219-20.

23 MacLeod (1934) p.108.

24 For the following account of Con's activities see Matheson (1970) pp.219-20.

25 *Historical Manuscripts Commission* (HMC) *14th Report Appendix Part III The Marchmont MSS* London 1894 pp.135-36 no.191 Letter from Sir James Ogilvie, Whitehall, to Earl of Marchmont 23 Sept. 1697.

26 *HMC 12th Report Appendix Part VIII* The Manuscripts of the Duke of Athole London 1891 p.55 no.139 Letter from Sir James Steuart, Lord Advocate, Edinburgh, to Earl of Tullibardine 21 Oct. 1697.

27 HMC Athole p.56 no.142 Letter from Patrick Murray of Dollary, Edinburgh, to Earl of Tullibardine 27 Oct. 1697.

28 HMC Marchmont p.137 no.197 Letter from Earl of Tullibardine, Kensington 2 Nov. 1697.

29 HMC Marchmont p.147 no.217 Letter from Dr Cornelius Con 22 Dec. 1698.

30 HMC Marchmont pp.147-48.

31 J. MacCulloch *A Description of the Western Isles of Scotland, including the Isle of Man* London 1819 Vol.I p.209.

32 T.S. Muir *Characteristics of Old Church Architecture etc. in the Mainland and Western Isles of Scotland* Edinburgh 1861 pp.191-92.

33 Muir (1861) pp.198-99.

34 Muir (1861) pp.192-94.

35 Repair work was apparently carried out in 1959 by J.M. Boyd and J.D. Lockie (Seabirds at Sea Team: *The birds of North Rona and Sula Sgeir* Nature Conservancy Council 1989 p.10).

36 *Ordnance Survey* (OS) *Name Book* (NB) no.136 p.40 Scottish Record Office SRO RH4/23/165.

37 CWC MS 115 Notes of Information from Angus Gunn.

38 CWC MS 230 "North Roney".

39 CWC MS 230 "Notes for Mr Carmichael 7 December 1885".

40 Munro pp.87-88.

41 G. Buchanan *Historia Scotorum* 1582.
cf. Balfour's Collection f.362: "South east [i.e. north east] from Lewis almost 60 myles Layes the Iyland Rona Low plane and verey fertile veill mannurat the Lord of it allotts, So maney houshouds to occupay it, appoynting for everey houshold few or maney Sheipe at his plesur quheron they may easily live and pay his rent: In this Iyle ther is a Chapell dedicated to St Ronan, querin (as aged men report) ther is alwayes a Spade found quher quhen aney is dead with it they find the place of his Grave marked besydes other fishes in this Iyland ther is about it grate plenty of Whales".

42 Accounts of Whales, Fishing etc. NLS Advocates Manuscript 33.5.16f.57 (p.99). See J. Aikman's translation of Buchanan (Glasgow 1827) Vol.I pp.54-55.

43 See n.42.
44 *Calendar of State Papers relating to Scotland etc.* (CSP) Vol.XI (1936) p.253.
45 CSP Vol.XII (1952) p.172 no.143 21 March 1596 (Copy of 1593 paper).
46 *"The Description of the Isles of Scotland"* NLS Advocates Manuscript 31.2.6 p.24. See also J. Skene *Celtic Scotland* Edinburgh 1880 Vol.III p.431.
47 *Acts of the Parliament of Scotland* (APS) Vol.IV pp.160-61.
48 *Register of the Great Seal* 1634-51 Vol.IX p.241 no.672.
49 APS Vol.VIII pp.382-83.
50 Matheson (1970) p.206.
51 See n.19.
52 See n.19.
53 See n.16.
54 See n.16.
55 See n.21.
56 MacLeod (1934) p.104.
57 MacLeod (1934) p.104.
58 The following account is derived from the *Morrison Manuscripts* Vol. no.8 in Stornoway Public Library. See also N.M. MacDonald (editor) *The Morrison Manuscript — Traditions of the Western Isles* Stornoway 1975 pp.287-90; *Stornoway Gazette* 4 September 1976 Article: "Tales and Traditions of the Western Isles" by N.M. MacDonald. MacDonald (1975) gives "Rona-a-taiff" incorrectly as "Rona a Tuath".
59 See n.19.
60 MacLeod (1934) p.104.
61 OSNB no.136 p.7.
62 MacCulloch (1819) Vol.I p.207.
63 J. MacCulloch *The Highlands and Western Isles of Scotland* London 1824 Vol.III p.312.
64 OSNB No.136 p.8.
65 J. Walker *An Economical History of the Hebrides and Highlands of Scotland* Edinburgh 1808 Vol.I p.23.
66 J. Sinclair (editor) *The Statistical Account of Scotland 1791-99* (OSA) Reprint Wakefield 1983 Vol.XX The Western Isles p.9.
67 OSNB no.136 p.8.
68 J.W. Dougal *Island Memories* Edinburgh 1937 pp.132-33.
69 OSNB no.136 p.8.
70 OSA p.9.
71 This account of the Murrays is mainly derived from Ness tradition and from W. Matheson "The Pape Riot and its sequel in Lewis" in *Transactions of the Gaelic Society of Inverness* Vol.XLVIII (1972-74) Inverness 1976 pp.395-434.
72 Matheson (1976) suggests a "more prosaic" origin for "gorm"; Murray's appearance may have been "swarthy or raven-haired" (p.401).
73 It was said that An Gobha Gorm "obtained the raw material of his craft by smelting the bog iron which was plentiful in Lewis in those days". There was also a belief that he was endowed with supernatural powers, his skill being given to him by the fairies. One later explanation for this was that he had "acquired this reputation because he was the first blacksmith in Lewis to use a certain amount of coal instead of peat charcoal. The coal was secretly imported and enabled him to weld where other blacksmiths in Lewis had to use rivets" (Matheson 1976 pp.399-400).
74 *Gillanders of Highfield Papers* (GHP) SRO GD 427/1/1 My Lords Rental of the Lewis Island 1740.
75 GHP 4/1-2, 5/5, 8/1, 9/1 Rentals. The rent for Swainbost and Rona rose from £24 in 1755 to £30.3s.4d in 1766, was increased to £33 in 1779-80 (13/4), and again in 1787 to £39.15s (15/2).

76 GHP 2/1 Judicial Rental 1754. A note of "Entries" paid at "the last Sett" 1752 includes £4.6s for "the Island of Rona" (GHP 28).

77 John Murray had a share of the tack earlier than this, but perhaps only temporarily. In the 1766 "Minute of Sett of the Island of Lewis" the mother, Elizabeth Mackenzie, "Rory and John Morrays" all agreed "to take the farms of Swanybost and Island Rona" at the annual rent of £30.3s.4d sterling (GHP 34).

78 *Seaforth Papers* SRO GD 46/6/24 "A list of the families and number of persons in each family in the Parish of Ness" January 1792.

79 *Lewis Estate Rental Books* (LERB) in Stornoway Public Library Vol.I 562/30.

80 LERB Vol.I 565.

81 LERB Vol.II 522.

82 LERB Vol.II 522.

83 LERB Vol.I 522, 541.

84 LERB Vol.II 593.

85 LERB Vol.II (loose paper) Letter from Farquhar Murray, North Dell, 28 January 1892.

86 LERB Vol.I 563.

87 R. Atkinson *Island Going* London 1949 p.88.

88 Muir (1861) p.201.

89 See n.85.

90 CWC MS 230.

91 For information on this family see LERB. I am also indebted to Bill Lawson, Harris.

92 It is also suggested that he married a daughter of Norman MacLeod, tacksman of Dalbeg in Lewis (Matheson 1976 p.417).

93 Another possible ancestor or at least close relation was "Murdo Mcfinlay Roy", one of the tenants in Swainbost who gave evidence in 1754 (see n.76).

94 Muir (1861) p.192.

95 Muir (1861) p.198.

96 Muir (1861) pp.199-200.

97 Muir (1861) p.198.

98 MacCulloch (1819) Vol.I p.207. MacCulloch also says that the *Fortunée* visited when "employed in cruising after the President in 1812", but, according to the ship's log, Rona was approached on 24 July 1813 (see p.00 below).

99 MacCulloch (1819) Vol.I p.204.

100 MacCulloch (1819) Vol.I p.204.

101 MacCulloch (1819) Vol.I p.205.

102 MacCulloch (1824) Vol.III pp.308-9.

103 MacCulloch (1819) Vol.I p.206.

104 MacCulloch (1819) Vol.I p.206.

105 MacCulloch (1824) Vol.III p.311.

106 MacCulloch (1824) Vol.III p.310.

107 MacCulloch (1819) Vol.I p.207n.

108 MacCulloch (1824) Vol.III p.311.

109 MacCulloch (1819) Vol.I p.207.

110 MacCulloch (1824) Vol.III p.315.

111 MacCulloch (1819) Vol.I p.207.

112 MacCulloch (1824) Vol.III pp.315-16.

113 MacCulloch says that the feathers were the produce of the gannets; but he may have been mistaken as it is unlikely that gannets then nested on Rona and MacCagie had no boat to get to Sula Sgeir. In 1764 38 stones of feathers came from Sula Sgeir, Rona and the Flannans and these seem to have been mostly eider down — see M.M. McKay (editor) *The Rev Dr John Walker's Report on the Hebrides of 1764 and 1771* Edinburgh 1980 pp.42, 48.

114 MacCulloch (1824) Vol.III p.318.
115 MacCulloch (1819) Vol.I p.209.
116 MacCulloch (1824) Vol.III p.317.
117 MacCulloch (1819) Vol.I p.207.
118 MacCulloch (1819) Vol.I p.209.
119 MacCulloch (1819) Vol.I pp.208-9.
120 MacCulloch (1819) Vol.I pp.208-9.
121 MacCulloch (1819) Vol.I p.209.
122 MacCulloch (1824) Vol.III p.320.
123 MacCulloch (1824) Vol.III p.317.
124 MacCulloch (1824) Vol.III pp.317-18.
125 MacCulloch (1824) Vol.III p.316.
126 MacCulloch (1819) Vol.I p.208.
127 MacCulloch (1819) Vol.I p.208.
128 MacCulloch (1824) Vol.III p.318.
129 MacCulloch (1819) Vol.I p.209.
130 MacCulloch (1819) Vol.I pp.209-10.
131 MacCulloch (1824) Vol.III pp.315-16.
132 MacCulloch (1819) Vol.I p.205.
133 MacCulloch (1819) Vol.I p.211.
134 MacCulloch (1824) Vol.III p.322.
135 CWC MS 230.
136 Matheson (1976) p.412) gives a version of the story which he found in the Stornoway Gazette and quotes:
"Saoil sibh féin nach mór an nàire
dh'fhear a leughas Beurla 's Gàidhlig
dhol a dh'éigheach ormsa 'Mheairlich'
air son na bhàth Gèo Mèadhar"
137 Matheson remarks on a connection between the name "Somhairle" and certain MacKays (1976 pp.407-8). The early Iain Ruadh MacPhàil (McKay) was in Uig traditions known as Iain mac Shomhairle. Iain Ruadh did not have a father called Somhairle, and there is no reason to suppose that Murdo did either. Furthermore there were, and perhaps still are, in Lewis "some families called MacKay in English but *Clann Mhic Shomhairle* in Gaelic", one of which lived in Swainbost. Whether Fionnlagh Ruadh, Murchadh Mac Shomhairle, "Murdo Mcfinlay Roy" (see n.93) and Iain Ruadh MacPhàil (Iain mac Shomhairle) were in fact related is uncertain, but Swainbost and the names of MacKay, Ruadh and mac Shomhairle seem to indicate a possible link.
138 For much information on the "Buidhe" family I am particularly indebted to Finlay MacLeod, Shawbost, the late Donald MacDonald, North Tolsta and Edinburgh, the late Alan MacDonald (Stugan), Cross, and the late Norman MacKay (Tormod Beag), Skigersta.
139 In a talk given about 1939 Angus L. MacDonald said that he knew Iain Buidhe "who was born on Rona":
"Chunnaic mi fhéin ann an Nis fear, Iain Buidhe, a chaidh a bhreith ann an Rònaidh. Bha e 'na fhior sheann duine agus bha mise am bhalach, ach tha cuimhne agam gun dubhairt e gun deidheadh e air ais do Rònaidh gu toilichte — nach robh àite air an t-saoghal a b'fhearr leis".
(I myself saw in Ness a man, Iain Buidhe, who was born in Rona. He was then an old man and I was a boy, but I remember him saying that he would happily return to Rona — that it was his favourite place in the world.)
(The manuscript text of the talk is in private possession).
140 Seaforth Papers Vol.70.
141 CWC MS 230 for the recollections of Murdo MacDonald and Iain Buidhe.

142 LERB Vol.III 580.
143 LERB Vol.IV 539.
144 LERB Vol.II 612-613.
145 LERB Vol.II 612-613.
146 OSNB no.136 p.8.
147 CWC MS 230 Notes for Mr Carmichael 7 December 1885.
148 CWC MS 230.
149 CWC MS 230.
150 M. Stewart *Ronay* London 1933 p.6.
151 OSNB no.136 p.16. It was also remarked that "articles of any weigh[t] may be landed in perfect safety by means of small Boats, when the wind is from the W. or S.W.".
152 OSNB no.136 p.37.
153 Hydrographic Survey records, Ministry of Defence, Taunton.
154 R. Pitcairn *Criminal Trials in Scotland* Edinburgh 1833 Vol.3 pp.109-110.
155 Notes from the log of HMS Fortunée (Admiralty 51/2381/7) kindly supplied by Mr Robert Atkinson.
156 CWC MS 230.
157 CWC MS 230.
158 CWC MS 362.
159 OSNB no.136 pp.5-40, 81-90.
160 T.S. Muir *Ecclesiological Notes on some of the Islands of Scotland* Edinburgh 1885 pp.87-89.
     Although he omitted part and made other alterations, Muir's original was a printed report signed by Captain R. Burnaby R.E., and dated 3 February 1852. This report was used, and even perhaps prepared, as background information in support of a proposal to turn Rona into a penal settlement (see p.89). The Muir/Burnaby version appeared again in 1888 (J.A. Harvie-Brown and T.E. Buckley *A Vertebrate Fauna of The Outer Hebrides* Edinburgh 1888 pp.xlii-xliv), apparently from the Burnaby report but with much more omitted, and it was noted (p.xliv) that the "Original, dated 1850", was to be seen in the "Ordnance Survey Office, Southampton". There are differences between the Burnaby report of 3 February 1852 and the description of the island written into the namebook on which it is based, for which reason the latter is included in full as an appendix on pages 173-174.
161 OSNB no.136 pp.6-7.
162 OSNB no.136 p.7.
163 The map and accompanying paper were kindly made available by Mr Peter K. Clark, Keeper, Map Room, Royal Geographical Society, London.
164 Muir (1885) p.89.
165 Muir (1861) pp.189-90.
166 Muir (1861) p.189.
167 Muir (1885) p.90.
168 Muir (1885) pp.90-91.
169 Muir (1861) p.200.
170 Muir (1885) p.91.
171 Muir (1885) p.91.
172 Muir (1861) pp.200-201. The Stornoway schoolmaster went along "to kill scarts" in this account, but later Muir said that his purpose was "to take a shot at the puffins" (1885) p.93.
173 Muir (1861) p.201, (1885) p.91. The subsequent account of activities derives from these two sources.
174 OSNB no.136 p.37.
175 OSNB no.136 pp.33-34, 81.

176 OSNB no.136 p.20.
177 MacCulloch (1824) Vol.III p.310.
178 OSNB no.136 p.14.
179 Muir (1861) p.198n.
180 CWC MS 230 "North Roney".
181 CWC MS 230 "North Roney".
182 See M. MacPhail "Folklore from the Hebrides II" in *Folklore* Vol.VIII (1897) pp.384-85.
183 Muir (1861) pp.197-99. The *west* gable wall of the chapel collapsed during the 1986-87 winter. (The birds of North Rona etc. p.10).
184 For Swinburne's account of his visit to Rona see *Proceedings of the Royal Physical Society of Edinburgh* Vol.VIII (1883-84) pp.51-67, but quoted here from the version given by Harvie-Brown and Buckley pp.xxxv-xlv.
185 Harvie-Brown and Buckley p.xlv.
186 Other than tradition, sources for the following account include CWC MS 230 Notes for Mr Carmichael, newspaper cuttings etc.; J.A. Harvie-Brown "Further Notes on North Rona, being an Appendix to Mr John Swinburne's Paper on that Island in the 'Proceedings' of this Society, 1883-84" in *Proceedings of the Royal Physical Society of Edinburgh* 1885-88 pp.284-89 (largely based on information supplied by Alexander Carmichael); Harvie-Brown and Buckley p.li; Dougal p.157.
187 CWC MS 230 Notes for Mr Carmichael. Harvie-Brown (Further Notes p.285) says that a boat went out in September and "the friends endeavoured to get the two men to return to their families and friends, but in vain".
188 The source of this account is a collection of papers in the *Stornoway Sheriff Court Processes* SRO SC33/42/11-12.
189 For Harvie-Brown's descriptions of his visits to Rona see Harvie-Brown (Further Notes etc.), Harvie-Brown and Buckley (1888), MS Journals of J.A. Harvie-Brown (formerly held by the Nature Conservancy Council, by whose permission they were consulted, and now by the National Museums of Scotland S/1883 pp.32-33 and 1885 pp.453, 471, 473-498).
190 See Duchess of Bedford "On visits paid to the island of N. Rona" in *Annals of Scottish Natural History* 1910 pp.212-214; "Spring bird-notes from various Scottish islands" in *Scottish Naturalist* 1914 pp.173-181.
191 Stornoway Gazette 13 June 1917.
192 The Royal Commission on Ancient and Historical Monuments and Constructions in Scotland: *Ninth Report with Inventory of Monuments and Constructions in the Outer Hebrides, Skye and the Small Isles*, Edinburgh 1928 pp.3-4.
193 For the account of his visit see Dougal pp.150-64; Stornoway Gazette 12 August 1927 Article: "Visit to Rona. Interesting Facts Brought to Light" by J.W.
194 Helen Dougal *Natural Resources of Lewis* Unpublished dissertation for Diploma in Geography, University of Edinburgh 1928 (Copy in Stornoway Public Library) p.24.
195 See Stewart pp.1-4.
196 See Atkinson (1949) pp.145-48.
197 F.F. Darling *Island Years* London 1940 p.261. For this account of Darling's visits to Rona see Island Years pp.240-45, and his *A Naturalist on Rona* Oxford 1939 pp.48-49.
198 R. Atkinson *Shillay and the Seals* London 1980 pp.125-128.
199 *Glasgow Herald* 18 July 1959.
200 *The Orcadian* 14 February 1963.
201 *Sunday Express* 24 February 1963.
202 In November 1887 Angus Morrison, Swainbost, told Carmichael that "The seals

used to cub in Sùlasgeir, not in Rona, as this was inhabited" (Carmina Gadelica Vol.IV Edinburgh 1941 p.12).

203 Harvie-Brown and Buckley pp.24-25.
204 CWC MS 230.
205 *The Northern Weekly* 30 September 1897 Article: "North Rona and its seals".
206 Dougal p.159.
207 Dougal pp.158-59.
208 CWC MS 112 p.211.
209 Harvie-Brown and Buckley p.xlv.
210 CWC MS 230.
211 See n.85.
212 Dougal p.151.
213 Atkinson (1949) pp.88-90.
214 Atkinson (1949) pp.178-83.
215 Darling (1940) pp.263-66.
216 MacLeod (1934) p.103.
217 MacLeod (1934) p.104.

APPENDIX I
Rona

In the Atlantic Ocean, off the northern coast of Scotland, in Latitude 59 7' 15" 48N and Longitude 5° 48' 50" West.

This Island forms part of the Lewis property and lies about 38 miles N.East of the Butt of Lewis, with which and Cape Rath it forms a triangle which is nearly equilateral. From its highest point which is nearly 360 feet above the level of the Sea Cape Rath, a considerable portion of the neighbouring shore, and some of the Lewis and Harris hills can on a clear day be distinctly seen without the aid of Glasses. In figure it bears a striking resemblance to a long-necked glass Decanter with the neck towards the North. Its greatest length is nearly one mile, its greatest breadth the same. At its North end there is a portion of about half a mile in length, which varies in breadth from ten to twenty chains, about half of this portion is composed of stratified rock without a particle of vegetation. This is the lowest part of the Island, its Eastern shore sloping gently to the sea and its western one though rugged and broken, not more than 90 feet in altitude. The southern portion is broader and more elevated — the largest part of it being ¾ of a mile broad — and the two hills on the East and West not less than 350 feet high — that on the East being the higher of the two by about 40 feet. The seaward bases of both these hills form steep precipitous cliffs, which in many places are inaccessible. The rocks around Rona are few and small — the only ones which are more than two chains from the shore being Gouldig Beag and Gouldig Mhor — the latter is about half a mile south of the S. East point of the Island, and the other is between *that* and the Shore. There is another small rock, seen only at L.W. near the S.W. point which is dangerous to navigators who may attempt to cast anchor in its neighbourhood. The soil of Rona is good — and the pasture though not luxuriant is beautifully green — indeed the whole Island, with the exception of about 50 acres, may be considered arable land interspersed with a few small rocks and numerous small piles of stones. A small portion on the Southern side appears to have been cultivated and has it is said yielded excellent Barley. It is now rented by a farmer from Lewis as a sheep farm and it feeds about 200 sheep at present. There are five or six rude, flat-roofed ruinous huts on it, the neatest and smallest of which is said to have been a church. There is also a graveyard here in which there is a rude stone Cross without any inscription. There are neither Rats nor Mice, and but very few Birds on it. It has no peat moss and not much seaweed. There is a sufficiency of Spring water on its southern shore.

Seals are very numerous here but not easily Killed, and Codfish abound around its Coast. The tides rise from 5 to 10 feet, and the prevailing wind is from the South West.

The best landing places are Poul Houtham on the South, Skildiga on the West, and Geodh Sthu on the East, the first and last being much superior to the other both for safety and accommodation. The most favourable winds are, for Poul Houthan, a Northerly or Easterly wind, for Geodh Sthu a Southerly or Westerly one, and for Skildiga a Southerly or Easterly one. So well sheltered is Geodh Sthu, that three vessels have been known to cast anchor at its mouth about six years ago. They remained during one night, but it is said that such had not previously occurred, nor has it been since repeated. Articles of any weight may be safely landed at Rona providing the weather is moderate, but the small Boat, which must be used on such a duty, should invariably be drawn up on the shore after use, and for this purpose ten men will be sufficient for a boat of 24 feet Keel. Dnd McLeod (commonly styled 'King of Rona') states that it is a well sustained and correct tradition that six men with their wives and families resided here about 200 years ago, and that the men when on a Seal excursion were drowned in Poll Halher, on the Southern shore of Rona. Their families after remaining on the island for six months after the catastrophe were brought to the Lewis, by the Boats which then annually visited the Island. The next person who inhabited it is said to have been a female in whose favour a miracle had been wrought under the following circumstances. It being an old and well received tradition in the Lewis that 'Fire never quenched on Rona' this dame resolved to test its truth but to her consternation found it to be a fallacy — however after offering up some fervant prayers her fire was relighted by supernatural agency. After this occurrence it was inhabited from time to time by individuals to whom nothing remarkable occurred though some of them resided on it for 5 and some, 7 years — but it is broadly hinted by some of the peasantry, that there now resides at Ness a woman who was transported from Lewis to Rona about 40 years ago — whether for theft or general bad conduct, is not generally Known. It is even said that a man was transported from Rona to Sulisker for sheep stealing and that he died on the latter place for want of sustenance. Donald McLeod *King of Rona* was its last human inhabitant — he resided there about 6 years ago for a period of 12 months — he appears to have been weary of his solitude and expresses a horror at the idea of being left there again. His residence on Rona, together with his rude yet muscular figure, have procured him the above title.

OSNB no. 136 (SRO RH4/23/165) pp.5-8
The account is also given on pp65-55 of the Name Book where it is entitled 'Description of Rona by Corp. Hayes' and signed by Michael Hayes 2nd Corp. RSM'. It appears therefore that Captain Burnaby may merely have signed his name to an 'improved' version.

APPENDIX II

Place names of Rona
See page 179, appendix III, for the map showing the locations referred to in this list.

1.   EXACT LOCATIONS

	OS informant Donald Macleod	OS 1st. Edition 6" Map	Notes From Name Book
1.	Lisgar Mhor	Lisgear Mhòr	
2.	Bho na Lisgar	Boghannan Lisgear	
3.	Sgoir na Leaca Mhora	Sgor na Lice Mòire	'can be landed on in calm weather'.
4.	Geodh na Tol	Geadh' an Tuill	
5.	Leac Mhor Fianuis	Leac Mhòr Fianuis	'sea breaks over it furiously with an Easterly or Northerly wind'.
6.	Poul an Clearach	Pal' a' Chleirich	'A narrow creek forming two sides of a Triangle. Its southern cliff is about 90 feet high and its Northern Boundary is perpendicular'.
7.	Feenish	Fianuis	
8.	Longaberry	Langa Beirie	'A small creek ... good landing place in Calm weather'.
9.	Skildaga	Sgeildige	
10.	Geodh Sthu	Geodha a Stoth	'an excellent landing place'.
11.	Geodh Bla Beag	Geodha Blatha Beag	
12.	Geodh Leash	Geodha Lèis	
13.	Geodh Bla Meadhonach		
14.	Geodh Bla Mor	Geodha Blatha Mòr	
15.	Ton Braighe	Ton Breighe	
16.	Sithean a Croer		'A small green hill ...'
17.	Geodh Maire	Geodha Mairi	
18.	Geodh Smu		'A small creek'.
19.	Stron na Gaorach	Sròn nan Caorach	'The most prominent point'.
20.	Tho Rona	Toa Rona	'Tobha Rònaidh'.
21.	Leac an Taulure	Leac Iain Tailleir	'A portion of cliff'.
22.	Prigahaune Lamhachleit	Prigeachan Lamhacleit	"A large barren high water rock, on which seals are usually seen'.
23.	Lamhachleit	Lamha Cleit	
24.	Geodha an Brathan	Geodha na Breatuinn	'A small creek'.

175

25.	Poul Houtham	Poll Thothatom	'the safest and most commodious landing place' except for 'Geodh Sthu'.
26.	Chleit a Sunas	Cleit an t-Sionnaich	
27.	Na poutanisk	Pollan Uisge	
28.	Stron a Heintor	Sròn an t-Tinntir	
29.	Gouldig Beag	Gealldruig Bheag	
30.	Gouldig Mhor	Gealldruig Mhòr	'Seals resort to it in great numbers'.
31.	Harsgoir	Harsgeir	'A large flat barren rock on which is a Trigl. Station'.
32.	Caolas Harsgoir	Caolas Harsgeir	
33.	Lobasgoir	Lòba Sgeir	
34.	Cleit Domhnull Ruadh		'A small high water rock between Caolas Loba sgoir and Caolas Harsgoir'.
35.	Caolas Lobasgoir	Caolas Lòba Sgeir	
36.	Meircasta	Marcasgeo	
37.	Cladach Cro Eoin Dearg	Cladach Crò Iain Dheirg	
38.	Leaca Siara	Leacan's Iar	'A point of land which projects in a Northerly direction'.
39.	Scaple	Sceapull	'A small patch of arable land ... There are three small enclosures on it, the fences of which are built of stone, and about two feet in height'.
40.	Geodh na Gaul	Geodha nan Gall	
41.	Buaile na Sgrath	Buaile na Sgrath	'Turf Park'.
42.	Haccleit	Hacaclaid	
43.	Geodh Haccleit	Geodha Hacaclaid	
44.	Sgrobagan na Biast		
45.	Cro Eoin Cheannich	Crò Mhic Iain Choinnich	
46.	Bogha Meadhonla	Bogh' a Mheadhon La	'Signifies Mid-day Rock' — 'very dangerous for vessels'.
47.	Leac na Sgreup	Leac na Sgròb	'A sloping shelf of rocks'.
48.	Slochit a Prisan	Stoc a' Phriosain	
49.	Rudha Prisan		'A small point of land on the N. Western end of Heilleir'.
50.	Healleir	Heallair	
51.	Poll Heallir	Poll Heallair	
52.	Rona	Rona	'The ruins of a village of huts'.

Other sources.

53.	Ferrin a gowan (oral tradition)
54.	Leathad Fhianuis (oral tradition)
55.	Mullach a' Bhaile (MacDonald - see 3 &4 below)
56	Fuaran Hjallr (MacDonald - see 3 &4 below)

2.   APPROXIMATE LOCATIONS

Donald Macleod	1st. Edition 6" Map	Notes From Name Book
57. Geodh an Dulisg		'There is abundance of Dilse'.
58. Geodh Caomhag		'A small rocky creek'.
59. Loch Shient		'A small salt water loch or pool ... It appears to be supplied by the spray, and sometimes by hole sheets of water, thrown into it from the Sea'.
60. Geodh Mhic Reekal		'Nicolson's creek'. 'A small rocky creek'.
61. Feegah		'A small creek'.
62. Poul Shote		
63. Geodh Fallasgair		'Next to and west of Geodh na Gaul'.

3. Names (22 in all) which are versions of those in list 1 and 2. They are numbered to allow comparison.*

7.	Fianuis (Leathad)	30.	Gealltrigeal (or 29)
9.	Skeildigja	33.	Lòpa-sgeir
10.	Sto (th)	36.	Miorcisgya
12.	Geodha Leid	40.	Geodha nan Gall
14.	Geodha Bladha	44.	Scròbag nam Biasd
15.	Ton-Brèidhe	46.	Bodha a' Mheadhon-Latha
16.	An Sithean	48.	Slochd a' Phriosain
17.	Geodha Mèithr (Meur)	50.	Hjallr (sgur, fuaran)
20.	An Tòdha	58.	Geodha Caomhag
21.	Palla na Saile	61	Fridhaigya
25.	Ho-a-tom	62	Poll Sgad

4. These are additional to lists one and two but are of uncertain location.*

	MacDonald	Recently Recorded
64.	Birra-Brat	
65.	An Caolas Siar	
66.	Radhaigya	
67.	An Cambar	
68.	Lidhe Theadhair	'Hageir'.
69.	Lidhe an t-Sithein	'Heehan'.
70.	Poll Thanga	
71.	Mullach Fjall	
72.	Bogha Stiubh-ard	

73.	Cro Fhionnlaidh	
74.	Stron nan Colcachan	
75.	Leabaidh Chaluim 'ic Fhionnlaidh	'Palla Chaluim 'ic Fhionnlaidh'.
76.	Cnoc nan Gall	?'Cnoc a Bhucanaich'.
78.	Talamh a Chairn	
79.	Skifgin	
80.	Fuaran Ho-a-tom	
81.	Fuaran Theirbaist	

* From Rona place names collected by Angus L MacDonald 'from Angus Gunn and Murdo MacDonald, Lionel, Ness, Lewis — 22.8.(19)23 and later'. The names are recorded in a form of spelling intended to reflect pronunciation and many differ from the O.S. map.

5. Dougal, P. 159 — refers to Gaelic names for land features.
(Numbers refer to lists 1&2).

'the slope of the fox' (26?) 'the house of Kenneth John's son' (45?)
'the nose of the sheep' (19) 'the slab of John the sailor' (21)
'the western Ledge' (38) 'the field of long grass' (?)
'Mary's boy' (17?)

(For further names see song on page 62)

APPENDIX III

The island of Rona showing placenames and
indication only of buildings and walls.

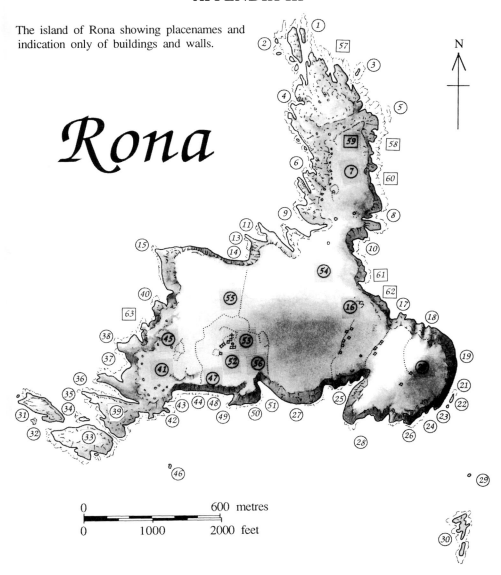

Rona

N

0 ___ 600 metres

0 ___ 1000 ___ 2000 feet